FAMILY REUNION

Making Peace
in the Jewish Community

BOOKS BY DANNY SIEGEL

Essays

1980 - ANGELS (out of print)

1982 - GYM SHOES AND IRISES
(Personalized Tzedakah)

1987 - GYM SHOES AND IRISES - BOOK TWO

1988 - MUNBAZ II AND OTHER MITZVAH HEROES

1989 - FAMILY REUNION:
Making Peace in the Jewish Community

Poetry

1969 - SOULSTONED (out of print)

1976 - AND GOD BRAIDED EVE'S HAIR (out of print)

1978 - BETWEEN DUST AND DANCE (out of print)

1980 - NINE ENTERED PARADISE ALIVE (out of print)

1983 - UNLOCKED DOORS
(An Anthology)

1985 - THE GARDEN:
Where Wolves and Lions Do No Harm
to the Sheep and the Deer

1985 - THE LORD IS A WHISPER AT MIDNIGHT
(Psalms and Prayers)

1986 - BEFORE OUR VERY EYES
Readings for a Journey Through Israel

Midrash and Halachah

1983 - WHERE HEAVEN AND EARTH TOUCH
(Book One)

1984 - WHERE HEAVEN AND EARTH TOUCH
(Book Two)

1985 - WHERE HEAVEN AND EARTH TOUCH
(Book Three)

1985 - WHERE HEAVEN AND EARTH TOUCH
SOURCE BOOK
(Selected Hebrew and Aramaic Sources)

1988 - WHERE HEAVEN AND EARTH TOUCH
(Combined Volumes: Books One, Two and Three)

1989 - WHERE HEAVEN AND EARTH TOUCH
(Combined Volumes) in Hardbound Edition

Humor

1982 - THE UNORTHODOX BOOK OF JEWISH
RECORDS AND LISTS
(With Allan Gould)

FAMILY REUNION

Making Peace
in the Jewish Community

Sources and Resources from
Tanach, Halachah and Midrash

by DANNY SIEGEL

THE TOWN HOUSE PRESS

Spring Valley, New York

I wish to express my thanks to the following people who helped me with this book:

To Professor David Goodblatt, Dr. Gordon and Myra Gondos, Michael and Joyce Bohnen, Moshe Waldoks, Dennis Brumberg, Mark Stadler, Mark Rotenberg, Jack Gruenberg, Jacob Staub, and Rabbis Peter Mehler, Jonathan Porath, and Aaron Mackler, and the people of the Shalva Jewish battered women's shelter in Chicago for discussing with me many critical points as I was developing the commentaries for this book and/or for supplying me with research materials.

To Dr. Arthur Green for sharing with me his speech from the General Assembly of the Council of Jewish Federations in New Orleans, November, 1988, which helped me focus on some of the essential issues. Even more important — for sharing the tale of Rabbi Raphael of Bershad which sets the tone for this book, and for offering additional insights into the tales of the Chassidic Rebbis.

To Mrs. Trude Holzmann of Denver, CO, who for the last few years has scanned a variety of newspapers and magazines, clipping and sending me articles which have afforded me the opportunity to extend and expand my comparisons between Torah and "real life".

To Edythe Siegel ("Mom"), former ace reporter for the *Asbury Park Press,* for proofreading the manuscript.

To Louise Cohen, for giving me the <u>Family Reunion</u> part of the title of the book.

Library of Congress Catalogue Card Number: 89-51212
International Standard Book Number: 0-940653-24-9

First Printing, 1989.

Cover by Allan Sugarman.

For ordering:
The Town House Press
28 Midway Road, Spring Valley, NY 10977

For Rabbi Steven Glazer,
my good friend
and gentle and patient teacher.

The Chassidic Master, Raphael of Bershad, was about to set out on a journey. A number of his followers decided to go along, and they sat down in the wagon with him.

As they were about to depart, yet another student said he wanted to join them, but the other students protested, saying the coach was already too crowded.

Listening to the exchange, the Master said, "Then we will just have to love each other that much more."

TABLE OF CONTENTS

INTRODUCTION

This is a time of crisis.

Whether or not this is a time of major crisis, or minor crisis, or medium-size crisis is not clear, but disunity and polarization within the community is in the news — and in the daily goings-on of the people. This volume is an attempt to bring to light Jewish sources which are a part of our classical literature, and which could be of use in any attempt to restore unity. Jewish literature *does* speak to these issues. That much is certain, but there are a couple of provisos:

1. The sources are often so high-sounding, they seem to exist only in the World of Ideals. They are impractical, unreal, unattainable by any normal person. In a number of the commentaries I try to deal with that problem.

2. The fact that so much of the literature sets this tone of unattainability or partial-reachability should not be discouraging. Nowhere do I state or even imply that there are vast numbers of people (myself most certainly included) living fully by these sources. There are, however, more and more concerned Jews who are trying in good faith to make headway, to clear the air, to sit down and attempt some solution(s). Maybe there are a half-dozen or so people I can think of who really have succeeded in reaching these levels of living; but there have always been just a few in that category. The rest must just use this good faith and honest openness to see how far they can go. Failure — even extensive (though not absolute) failure — comes with the turf.

The modern author Nikos Kazantzakis addresses the problem of high ideals and failure in Report to Greco. In one passage, he describes an encounter with his grandfather. The young Kazantzakis says, "Give me a command, beloved grand-father." The old man replies, "Reach what you can, my child." Young Nikos is not satisfied with the answer and asks for a more difficult command. The elder replies, "Reach what you cannot!"

There is shortsightedness, highhandedness, arrogance, indignation (righteous and otherwise), dirty politics, ugliness, ignorance, cruelty, injustice, daily unpleasantries, recrimination, nastiness....and on and on, too long a list. It seems endless. But there are also courageous people, people of goodwill, insight-ful people, people of integrity and moral stature, and lovers of peace who have set their minds to repair the fractures in the Jewish People's unity. Let us not forget them, nor their attempts at peacemaking through seminars, conferences, negotia-tions, face-to-face encounters, compromises-with-integrity. To some degree, they are offsetting the negatives. Whether they and their efforts outnumber and out-weigh the other side is not clear. It seems that the dissension-sowers have the up-per hand, but that, too, is not clear.

Some of the parties are right, and some are wrong; some are absolutely right, and others absolutely wrong, and some, naturally enough, are partly right and partly wrong. But the issue is just as much "How do we live together, live well together, at peace with each other?" as it is a question of who is right or absolutely or partially right and who is wrong or absolutely or partially wrong.

Is the crisis solvable? Can these texts (and the words of Kazantzakis's Zeyde) bring us to reconciliation, to peace, to more free time and energy for other, more productive Mitzvahs? I believe the answer is yes. It is a mighty task, but not beyond our capabilities, we Nobel prize laureates, we discoverers of the polio vaccine, we founders and leaders of labor movements, we settlers in and successful adjusters to so many foreign lands, we flowerers of the Negev, we who have been Davids against much more frightening Goliaths than this one.

This is a painful book, and a book about pain:

1. Preparing the material, I understood that the texts raised a potential problem of hypocrisy. Here were sources that were part of my own tradition, texts I had shuffled aside or had not examined in the light of the issue of Hava'at Shalom-Peacemaking. Was I prepared to take them seriously enough to make more of an effort to live by these sources? As I went from text to text, I felt like it was Yom Kippur in December, a time to make self-examination. That is one kind of pain: people who would want to take this seriously would have to look inside themselves to see if they have been putting enough of their own energies into Peacemaking. I (as I am sure with all of us) succeed only partially. So often when we are angered by the actions of others, we see that the source of the anger is that we ourselves are guilty of doing the same. But, if we make good-faith attempts to change, then, at least, our partial success will have had some element of meaning.

2. The other pain is much more massive — the anguish of people in all sectors of the community who are suffering from the backbiting, insult-slinging, and sometimes malicious excommunicatory diatribes. I believe the real starting point of this book is similar to the writing I have done about the Mitzvah of Tzedakah: human suffering. As individuals, we have all felt pain. We have not liked it, and we have rejected the too-smooth occasional false wisdom of "Pain is instructive. We learn from it." As human beings, and as Jews, we ought not to cause pain to others. That says it as succinctly as possible.

In the final stages of writing this book, I recalled an incident at the podiatrist's office. My father, the General Practitioner of 45+ years, had sent me to the specialist because there was something wrong with my foot. When I stretched out on the table, sock removed, naked foot extended for examination, I explained to the doctor that I "was not very good with pain". I told him I had always been able to go to Daddy who handled my psychological pain as well as my physical problem, always with what seemed like a magic touch. Don't get me wrong — the specialist was a good man, but he just didn't understand the full measure of what I was saying. When he shot my foot with anesthesia, I thought I would hit the ceiling. I had never felt such enormous pain. I hated that moment then, I hated it a few days ago when I recalled it, and I hate it now when I have to write about it. That is why pain is the starting point of this volume. Why would we, how *could* we want to inflict similar feelings on others? And how could we oppose efforts to alleviate pain and suffering? Knowing the joy the that surgeon, the ophthalmologist, the endocrinologist, the internist have in bringing relief to their patients, would we not want to opt for that joyous feeling, too?

Healers all.

I have practical hopes for this book. It was never meant merely as an exercise in intellectual stimulation. I would hope it would contribute towards some real results:

1. That it would foster the use of moral force rather than coercion in bringing about more peace in the Jewish community.

2. That certain practical techniques presented in the texts and commentary could be of use in this quest for peace, essentially in the Jewish community, but also in other contexts.

3. That it would encourage educators to focus on the problems, on the texts, on the grand scheme of Jewish unity, so that students young and old alike would make this a critical part of their active lives as Jews. We need more Mevi'ay Shalom-Peacemakers.

4. That it would encourage us to attend and/or set up more seminars and conferences in a front-line attempt to further the peacemaking process. And that we attach ourselves to the Peacemakers of our day, become their students, learn from them and attempt to bring to actuality their wisdom and insight.

5. That we recognize that two areas of neutral-and-common ground can be Torah study and Mitzvah work, and that these serve to break down the walls that are dividing us. That we should share more study groups on this topic and any Torah-topic, and set up more joint Mitzvah projects whereby we do the Mitzvah work together, serving all. There are so many areas where this is already true today: In Israel, Yad Sarah's lending medical equipment to anyone and everyone, and volunteers working for them from all sectors of the community, the Jewish food banks and battered women's shelters and alcoholics groups, serving all, being served by all. Teaching Hebrew reading, much as my Rabbi, Noah Golinkin, is doing (even in one day). Who can be against teaching people to read Hebrew? Would this not be an ideal example of all-kinds-of-Jews serving all-kinds-of-Jews? There are so many possibilities in this area of Jewish life.

6. That we realize that small acts of peacemaking are not so small. First of all, we never know which small act is the opening for much larger ones. And secondly, no one knows how much the sum total of accumulated small acts of peace adds up to. It's not simple mathematical addition. The interplay is much more complex, each small act bouncing off others, moving hostilities further out of the arena, exploding myths into thin air, easing — enormously — in complicated interactive ways the aches and pains of those who suffer.

I am often struck by how the august term "Tikkun Olam-Fixing the World" uses the same root T-K-N that means to repair or fix even the simplest, smallest glitches. You use the very same word when you speak of fixing a switch or a refrigerator, putting oil on a squeaky door hinge, unclogging a drain, adjusting a valve, setting the timing on a carburetor. It is sublimity-made-real through simple acts. Whoever coined the phrase centuries ago was telling us how the entire world can be less screechy, less clogged, lighter, and more comfortable by an infinite array of apparently insignificant acts.

Finally, I would like to thank Alan Teperow, Executive Director of The Synagogue Council of Massachusetts. It was he who invited me to address a conference entitled "Ahavat Yisrael — The Challenge of Diversity in Jewish Life" at Brandeis University in April, 1989. The material in this book is based on what I prepared for that conference. Throughout the preparation period he enlightened me at every turn, offering his insights and peacemaking skills to help me shape the material appropriately for the task at hand.

Danny Siegel

KEY TERMS

Ahava-אהבה — Love

    Ahavat Yisrael-אהבת ישראל— Love of the Jews

    Ahavat Chinnam-אהבת חנם— Love for no particular reason at all

    Sinat Chinnam-שנאת חנם — Senseless hatred

Kavod-כבוד — Dignity, honor

    Kevod HaBriot-כבוד הבריות — Dignity of God's creatures

        Tzelem-צלם — Image [of God]

        Demut-דמות — Image [of God]

Klal Yisrael-כלל ישראל — The entirety of the Jewish People

Hava'at Shalom Bayn Adam LeChavayro-הבאת שלום בין אדם לחברו —
    Peacemaking

OPENING PRAYER FOR PEACE

Rabbi Yochanan used to pray:

May it be Your will, O Lord, my God,
*   and God of my ancestors,*
to grace our lives with love
*   and a feeling of the intimacy of all humanity*
and peace and friendship,
*   and may all our days succeed because we are hopeful,*
and may the borders of our lives overflow with students,
*   and may we enjoy our reward in Paradise,*
and arrange things so that we will have good hearts
*   and good friends,*
and allow us to awaken with our yearnings fulfilled,
*   and may You consider our wishes to be decent-and-good.*

*   (Jerusalem Talmud,*
*   Berachot 4:2)*

KAVOD-DIGNITY

Kavod is Dignity. It is also Respect. It would be worthwhile to list some of the things this word is associated with in Rabbinic Literature:

God
All of God's creations
The Torah
Parents
Friends
Guests
The Shabbat
The holidays
The Elderly
The Sages
Teachers (by students)
Students (by teachers)
Language and vocabulary
The dead
Other people's possessions
The congregation.

Furthermore, Kavod appears in association with a number of verbs which express its wide usage:

Linhog, LaChalok — to show respect to
Litbo'a — to insist on the honor of, take the side of
LeMachot — to intervene on behalf of
La'Asok — be involved in
LeHamir — to sell out
La'Akor — to uproot, dispose of
Lifgo'a, Lifgom — to damage, harm someone's dignity
LaChush — to have a sense of someone's dignity
LaChus — to be careful of someone's dignity
LiMchol — to surrender one's dignity
LaRedet — to become impoverished.

In addition, there are times in the Bible and Talmud when Kavod can mean much more, extending even to awesomeness, and majesty. The term for God's divine throne is "Kissay HaKavod", and the clouds that accompanied in our wanderings in the wilderness were called "Ananay Kavod" — "Clouds of Glory."

When Rabbi Eliezer was about to die,
all his students came and sat before him.

They said to him,
"Rabbeynu — our teacher — teach us only one thing."

He replied,
"My children, what can I teach you?
Every one of you go and be very careful of the dignity of others...."
(Derech Eretz Rabba 3)

There are numerous deathbed scenes described in Rabbinic Literature. From a stylistic standpoint, the text sets the stage for the teacher to pass on to his students the Great Essences that the Rebbi has learned from Life and Torah. There is high drama and emotion in the air. Time is short. What, indeed, will the Rebbi teach, knowing the impact will be so long-lasting, perhaps more memorable than anything the students may have ever learned from him?

Rabbi Eliezer's choice is not philosophical and abstract, but very down-to-earth and real: dignity is the essence, treating others decently, because they are people. He reinforces how much he expects this to be taken as a practical plan of action by emphasizing "Every one of you go and..." The grammatical form is imperative, a command. "Do it!" he says. "Each of you, every one of you; that is the best way to remember who I was alive."

1.

The Kavod-dignity of God's creatures is very great.

**(Berachot 19b,
First Translation)**

2.

How great is the Kavod-dignity of God's creatures!

**(Berachot 19b,
2nd Translation)**

3.

Ben Zoma says:
Who is worthy of being treated with honor [Mechubbad]?
One who [HaMechabbed] treats God's creatures with dignity.

(Pirke Avot 4:1)

The Talmudic phrase "Gadol Kevod HaBriot" carries the grammatical force of both translations 1 and 2. The former is descriptive — people are endowed with dignity, great dignity. The latter is more emphatic — awesome. In the second translation, it is as if someone has stood back at some moment and was struck simultaneously by the glory of so many phenomena: life (wondrous), people (miraculous), God's creativity (astounding)! Though the phrase appears in the Talmud usually in a Halachic-legal context, it also stands by itself as a succinct and eloquent theme-setter and point of departure for human activity.

The third text gives a refreshing view of the meaning of status, i.e., that status is determined not by high birth, not by profession or financial spreadsheets, but by how sharp a person's sense of human dignity is. Ben Zoma says that, when others sense that you have refined your grasp of human dignity, you will most certainly be treated honorably and decently.

The more one studies the word "Kavod" in all its forms, the more the student is taken by its range, texture, and depth. Indeed, it is easy to be overwhelmed by the thought that human beings can be both "Mechabbed-Capable of Making Kavod Happen" and "Mechubbad-A Worthy Recipient of Kavod".

"Love your neighbor as yourself," (Leviticus 19:18) —
Rabbi Akiva says,
"This is the all-encompassing Torah-principle."

Ben Azzai says,
"'This is the story of humanity:
[When God created the first human being,
He created that person in the likeness of God]' (Genesis 5:1)
is an even greater principle."

(Sifra, Kedoshim, on Leviticus 19:18)

It is not clear why Rabbi Akiva and Ben Azzai would attempt to lay down an Ultimate Principle. Both were fully aware of the dangers and shortcomings of this approach to dealing with an understanding of human beings, their place in the world, their relationship to God, the essence of inter-relationships: (a) any aphorism, proverb, single phrase would be incomplete, (b) over time, people would tend to abuse these principles, taking them out of context and bending them this way and that for their own immediate purposes, and (c) they, themselves, were living in — indeed, they were creating — the Talmudic Way of Thinking, which was based on an extensive detailing of everyday acts to clarify and embody whatever abstract principles would be discussed in the Torah academies.

On (c), though, perhaps they thought, at least, that immediately and inevitably people would call to mind Hillel's insight, "Anything you would hate to have done to you, do not do to others." Hillel must have seen a need, and by supporting their method with Hillel's name, they knew they had good precedent. Besides, Hillel had added, "The rest is commentary; now, go study!" Rabbi Akiva and Ben Azzai must have felt confident that their students would absorb these pieces of "Brief Torah", study the implications, and be motivated to action via the Halachic-Jewish legal framework of day-to-day action.

Rabbi Akiva's principle is, of course, the more eye-catching. First of all, he was the most distinguished teacher of his day (mid-1st Century-early 2nd-Century). And, secondly, the quote from Leviticus was already so well known it would most certainly be remembered and repeated. All he did, essentially, was say this is *the most basic* Jewish principle to live by.

Nevertheless, it appears that Ben Azzai's teaching is more all-encompassing. Logically speaking, if you hate yourself, then — according to Rabbi Akiva — you wouldn't have to love others. One could easily distort Rabbi Akiva's words to make them sound as if he were placing all of Judaism on your particular mood at a certain moment in time, i.e., when you are in a loving mood, then, surely, you will act lovingly towards others.

Ben Azzai's view, on the other hand, states a hard fact which stands independently on its own, unattached to any moment, passing frame of mind, or whim. He is saying, "This is Reality: Human beings are uniquely majestic, because they are created in God's image. They are — by the mere fact of being born — a reflection of God's Own Self. *They are endowed with innate Kavod-dignity, and because of that fact, they deserve to be treated by all others with Kavod-dignity."* As I have heard numerous students and friends discuss The Great Rabbi Akiva-Ben Azzai Debate, many find Ben Azzai's teaching more immediately effective as a reminder for Menschlich action. Considering the dignity of others demands a certain way of living. By comparison, "Love others as you love yourself" may be a bit too ethereal and hazy.

It must be clearly stated that, according to Ben Azzai, a person's worth is in no way dependent on his or her usefulness to society. A person with "special needs" is no less entitled to being treated with care and dignity than one who is so-called "normal". (In the final analysis, anyway, we all have special needs.) In ancient Greek culture it was not that way. According to the mores of that society, it was acceptable to "expose" children with defects. "Expose" literally means to "put out", i. e., to leave a "damaged" child out on some mountainside or some such place and allow them to die from "exposure". Such was to be the case with Oedipus. Oedipus's father, King Laius of Thebes, had learned from an oracle that a future son born to him and his wife Jocasta, would kill him. So he pierced his feet ("Oedipus" means "swollen foot"), and instructed a shepherd to leave him out on Mount Cithaeron. For whatever reason, the shepherd disobeyed the order, and Oedipus's subsequent life-story is told in many versions by the Greek tragedians. What jars us is that no one objected to the fact that King Laius decided to leave his own baby out on the mountain to die.

Returning to our text, it is interesting to note that of the two phrases, it is Rabbi Akiva's that has been made into a modern Hebrew song. One would wonder what would happen if someone wrote a Ben Azzai song, and did a controlled study of the two groups: the ones who sang Rabbi Akiva's version vs. Ben Azzai's, and whether or not the lasting effects on behavior would be greater for one group or the other.

In any event, for all the shortcomings of aphoristic Torah teaching, this text appears in a number of Rabbinic sources in different forms. It is quite clear that Rabbi Akiva's and Ben Azzai's discussion was well-known and thoroughly absorbed into the lives of individual Jews in their own day and in subsequent generations.

Today, their words are no less relevant.

The opposite views (and acting on those views) are seen daily and in varied areas of life. For example, a California winery refused to repair the shacks for the migrant grape pickers. The health department told them they would have to close down the buildings, which is what the company decided to do, leaving the workers to live outside. In response to abandoning the people to such unpleasant living conditions, one of the executives of the company said, "What makes these people so precious?"

Another example: a Nobel Prize Laureate's view of the preciousness of Human-Beings-As-Human-Beings — "No newborn infant should be declared human until it has passed certain tests regarding its genetic endowment and...if it fails these tests, it forfeits the right to live." (Francis Crick, quoted in *Playing God in the Nursery*, Jeffrey Lyon, pp. 198-199.)

In addition, modern medical research sadly provides numerous horrifying examples concerning human experimentation and informed consent:

1. Dr. John Rock, one of the primary developers of the contraceptive pill: "Some of his research has been called unethical. He has been criticized for conducting early tests of the Pill on mental patients without their consent, and for encouraging hysterectomy candidates to have intercourse before the operation without fully explaining that their excised organs would be searched for fertilized eggs." Sara Davidson in *Fifty Who Made the Difference*, p. 61.)

2. In the mid-1980's, the Food and Drug Administration caught 16 nursing homes in Phoenix testing new drugs on some of the residents, drugs that had not been approved by the FDA, and administered without the patients' consent. Some of the administrators of those homes were receiving kickbacks from the drug companies that wanted to test the drugs. (Article by Donald Robinson, *Parade Magazine*, August 16, 1987.)

3. Action was sought against the Director of the Illinois Department of Mental Health and Developmental Disabilities, the University of Chicago, and certain then-unknown drug companies to stop drug experimentation, adrenalectomies, and other procedures on state mental patients, without informed consent. Among those implicated was a Nobel Prize Laureate. (Documents from 1979, supplied to me by Patrick T. Murphy, Public Guardian of Cook County — the one who brought the action on behalf of the patients.)

4. In the 1980's: a physician/professor of medicine was teaching her students how to perform rectal examinations on mentally retarded young people in Kingston, Ontario, without any consent from family or guardians. A trial was held, the physician found guilty of assault, and the practice was stopped. (Article by Allan Gould in *Canadian Forum* Magazine, August/September, 1985.)

The final two cases are from a book called *A History and Theory of Informed Consent*, Ruth R. Faden and Tom L. Beauchamp (Oxford University Press, 1986), pages 161-162 and 165-167.

5. 1963, a chronic disease hospital in Brooklyn, NY: 22 patients receive "an injection of a suspension of foreign, live cancer cells". The patients already had cancer, but whatever the point of the experiment, it was determined to be non-therapeutic. No one on the staff tried to get the consent of the patients, and, indeed, some of them were incompetent to give such consent. After an investigation the practice was stopped.

6. The infamous Tuskegee Syphilis Study: Starting in 1932, under the aegis of the Public Health Service, a study took place tracing the development of syphilis in 400 black males. (200 men without syphilis were also observed as

"controls".) The men were never informed that the experiment was non-therapeutic, and any consent the men gave was manipulated by those conducting the study. At no time did the people in charge attempt to cure the men, and reports on the study appeared in major medical journals *as late as 1973*, even though a cure for syphilis had been found years — many years — before.

(It is unfortunate to have to note that a friend of mine, a rabbi who serves on a review board for a university hospital in his city, has a difficult time getting the researchers to *clearly* state the necessary and full information in their consent forms. He described to me his constant struggle to get the staff to lay out the consent forms in unequivocal language, so that the patient would know the exact details before agreeing to be a part of the experiment.)

I do not wish to single out the field of research for particular opprobrium. It just happens that this is an issue that has been of personal interest for a number of years, and I had gathered some material which I thought ought to be put together and presented in this context.

Enough said.

1.
"Other people's dignity should be as precious to you
as your own" (Pirke Avot 2:15) —
How is this to be understood?

This teaches that
a person should treat others with the same dignity
as he or she treats his or her own.

And just as no one wants
to have his or her own dignity trampled upon,
so, too, a person should not want
the dignity of others to be trampled upon.

(Avot DeRabbi Natan 15)

2.
Love other human beings and treat them with dignity.
Allow your wishes to be overridden by the wishes of others.

(Derech Eretz Zuta 1)

People are sensitive about — often touchy about — being treated with dignity. On a more practical plane, though, human beings recall much more clearly the times when they have felt hurt by someone for the wrong reasons, embarrassed or humiliated. It would appear that the strong point of text #1 is that, if people would recall now and again how unpleasant or painful moments of shame and embarrassment were in their own lives, they would most certainly avoid causing such feeling in others.

Text #2 adds yet another element: should a situation arise where a clash is imminent, where the stakes are high enough to cost someone his or her dignity, then we must be prepared to allow our own private needs or wishes to be set aside. This is a common-enough accommodation between spouses or between parents and children or friends-and-friends. The hard part is doing the same with acquaintances, strangers, and enemies.

Rabbi Nechunia ben HaKana's students asked him,
"To what do you attribute your longevity?"

He replied,
. . . .
[Among other things,]
"I never did anything
that would bring me honor
by humiliating someone else."

Rabbi Zera's students asked him,
"To what do you attribute your longevity?"

He replied,
. . . .
[Among other things,]
"I never found pleasure
in someone else's misfortunes or failures."

(Megillah 27b-28a)

Rabbinic literature doesn't simply state rules and regulations and offer inspirational messages. More often than not, the texts offer the student "Stories from Real Life". In this text, two Rabbis are asked about their personal lives, and we, the students, understand that honor, dignity, decency, and similar issues were taken very seriously. It is one thing to preach, it is another to be "Na'eh Doresh Ve'Na'eh MeKayyem-Living by the Words".

1.
One who curses oneself or another person...
transgresses a negative commandment.

(Shevu'ot 35a)

2.
No one should say,
"Just as I have been humiliated,
so, too, will I humiliate others."

Rabbi Tanchuma said:
If you do so,
know Whom you are humiliating,
[as the verse states] —
"He made him [Adam] in the likeness of God." (Genesis 5:1)

(Genesis Rabba 24, end
Buber 1:237)

Of supreme practical consequence is the issue of self-image. The first text puts the problem in Halachic-legal terms: we are not allowed to demean ourselves or treat our own selves with a lack of respect — because we are made in the Image of God. It is understandable on many grounds why we ought not to curse or degrade others, but the additional insight is how we should treat ourselves. We, as human beings, have Kavod, innate dignity. This text should strengthen us when we are confronted by people who try to take that dignity away....The text says that they cannot do that, and it is not for them to take it from us. (I have often said I wished I knew this before I went to college, for those painful occasions when a professor would indicate that not only was my work poor, but that *I* was somehow worth less because I had written such a poor paper or exam.)

The second text also makes sense in the context of our study of Human Dignity. The equation of Human Image=God's Image takes the often-agonizing event of humiliation out of the framework of purely human interpersonal relations. It is much more — an affront to the Creator.

1.
If we are in the presence of someone who is dying,
we are required to tear our garment at the moment of death.

What is this like?

It is like a Torah scroll that has been burned,
an occasion for which we are also required
to tear our garment.

(Mo'ed Katan 25a)

2.
At first,
they used to leave the faces of the bodies of the wealthy uncovered
and those of the faces of poor people covered.

But since the faces of the poor
were disfigured because of [hunger from] drought,
and the poor people feel humiliated,
they instituted the practice of covering everyone's face.

(Mo'ed Katan 27a)

3.
If a priest comes across a Met Mitzvah by the roadside,
he should ritually defile himself [and bury the body].

Even if he was a High Priest,
he is required to become ritually defiled and to bury him.

And what is a Met Mitzvah?
A Jew that was lying by the road
without anyone around to bury him.

(Maimonides, Mishna Torah,
Laws of Mourning 3:8)

Jewish mourning and burial practices demonstrate a further extension of the principles of Kavod-dignity.

Text #1 expands the practice of tearing a garment as a sign of mourning for the dead. This law is not talking about a relative who has died, but rather anyone. If we are present at the final moments of life, we are to tear our garment in recognition of the fact that something precious in this world has been lost, as precious as a Torah scroll that has been destroyed by fire.

Text #2 describes the origins of the present-day Jewish practice of a closed coffin: it was an embarrassment to poor people to display the disfigured faces of those who had suffered from hunger. (The Hebrew word for "disfigured" is "Mushcharim", which literally means "blackened".)

The third text is, I believe, the most striking of all. According to Jewish law, a Kohen-priest is not allowed to come into contact with dead bodies (except for the closest relatives). Dead bodies contaminate with Tum'ah, ritual impurity, which a Kohen was supposed to avoid, ostensibly at all costs....except in the case of an unclaimed body. What the text says is that it is so humiliating to have no one to bury you, that anyone and everyone should do it, even a High Priest.

Unfortunately, in modern American law, the opposite is very often the case. I have asked lawyers in various parts of the country to send me copies of local statutes concerning unclaimed bodies. My most recent one, from Richmond, VA, arrived just yesterday. The Code of Virginia, Health Code Article 3 ("Use of Dead Human Bodies for Scientific Study"), reads in part as follows:

§ 32.1-298. Notification of Commissioner and delivery of bodies. — Any person having charge or control of any dead human body which is unclaimed for disposition, which is required to be buried at the public expense, or which has been lawfully donated for scientific study shall notify the Commissioner whenever and as soon as any such body comes to his possession, charge or control and shall, without fee or reward, permit the Commissioner or his agents to remove such body, to be used for the advancement of health science.

§ 32.1-299. Distribution of Bodies. — A. The bodies received pursuant to §§ 32.1-298 and 32.1-288 shall be distributed by the Commissioner to institutions and individuals as they may be needed for the purposes of scientific education and training in health and related subjects as follows:

1. First, to the medical schools of Virginia.
2. Second....

No one denies the need for cadavers for medical training. There are those who explain that there is a shortage of available bodies for the students.

And yet, provision is made for people to "leave their bodies for science", as long as there are explicit instructions. At least from a Jewish standpoint, it seems diametrically opposed to the meaning of Kavod-dignity, that any person's body (particularly those of homeless people) should be used for these purposes, *unless specific instructions were left indicating that they wished their bodies used for medical purposes.* Rather than take advantage — even for the high purpose of medical advancement — of those who are at an ultimate disadvantage, Jewish tradition says we must go out of our way to provide those last fitting acts of decency and kindness — a dignified burial.

Finally, in some jurisdictions, the authorities may dispose of the unclaimed body within 36 hours.

Yet one more "finally", in many communities, the Jewish community makes it known to all appropriate agencies that they will provide free and proper burial for any Jews who die within their boundaries and have no one else to bury them.

Rabban Yochanan ben Zakkai said:

See how very great is the dignity of human beings:

For a [stolen] ox,
which walks on its own feet [when it is stolen —
the thief pays] fivefold compensation.

But for a [stolen] sheep,
which [the thief] has to carry on his shoulders —
[the penalty is only] fourfold.

(Bava Kamma 79b)

     A critical way to understand whether or not Jewish ideals were treated in any way as realistic and attainable is to study specific Halachot-laws. For example, if we recite Kiddush (the blessing over wine) in synagogue on Friday nights, there must be a reason, because it was assumed that everyone would do the same in his or her own home after congregational prayers were concluded. In fact, the Kiddush was recited in synagogue for the benefit of wayfarers who ate and drank and slept in the synagogue. Indeed, Rabbi Yosef Kapach, pre-eminent Yemenite Rabbinical scholar in Israel, indicates that synagogues in Yemen were built with the explicit condition that they would be used to house and feed wayfarers. Thus, in America today, with so many homeless and hungry people, there is good precedent for allowing synagogues to be used as soup kitchens and shelters.

     With our text of the ox and the sheep, we see the abstract principle of Kavod-Human Dignity concretized in the penal system. When a thief steals an ox, the fine is 500% of the value of the ox, but for a sheep it is only 400%. The reason is that the thief, having carried the sheep away on his shoulders, debased himself and surrendered his sense of Kavod. He already paid part of the price for his crime. Thus the reduction in the fine.

AHAVA-LOVE

Jewish literature abounds with terms for love, "Ahava" (the noun) and "Le'Ehov" (the verb) being just one of the roots. Other roots — covering many shades of meaning — include:

Chen
Chessed
Racham/Rachamim
Chavav/Chibev
Ratzah
Chamad.

Among the many things to be loved according to Jewish tradition are:

God
All Jews
Converts to Judaism
Strangers
All of God's creations
The Torah
The Land of Israel
Criticism
Tzedakah
Kindness (Chessed).

The opposite word, "Sin'ah" (the noun) and "Lisno" (the verb) can sometimes mean "hated", and other times "unloved", and yet other times some other closely-associated but distinct emotion or action. There are many kinds of "Sin'ah" in Jewish literature: open hate, hidden hate ("hate in the heart"), and the insidious "Sin'at Chinnam-Hate for No Decent Reason". The Chassidic Rebbi Yechezkel of Kuzhmir (died 1856) coined a counterbalancing term "Ahavat Chinnam-Love for No Particular Specific Reason". Rabbi Avraham Yitzchak Kook, the first Ashkenazi Chief Rabbi of modern Israel later popularized the term. Both felt there was the need for a term that could offset the commonly-known "Sin'at Chinnam".

One additional minor touch: the Me'am Lo'ez commentary to the Torah points out that the numerical value of the letters for "Ahava" equal the same number as "Echad", meaning "One"....Love and Unity are equal.

With this brief introduction, we will now explore some of the texts that will help us get a finer grasp of Ahava and Sin'ah, Love and Hate, in our centuries-old tradition.

This is what The Holy One blessed be He said to Israel,

"My children, have I deprived you in any way?
What do I want from you?

I only ask that you should love each other,
and treat each other with dignity,
and stand in awe of each other."

(Seder Eliahu Rabba 26)

A simple text.

A succinct text.

The two essential words are here: "Ahava-Love" and "Kavod-Dignity", plus a third element — "Yir'a-Awe".

Reversing the order of the clauses, it would make sense that, if (a) a person is awed by the essence and presence of another human being, then it would be natural to preserve the other's dignity and love that person.

And furthermore, the other person need not have an awesome personality, nor awesome achievements to his or her credit. It is enough that the Other One be human in order to deserve to be treated with dignity and love.

1.
Love others as you love yourself.

(Leviticus 19:18)

2.
Hillel said,
"....
Anything you would hate to have done to you,
do not do to others."

(Shabbat 31a)

The first text, straightforward and perhaps too-high-sounding.

The second text, according to some commentators (Torah Temimah, for example), yields a more realistic approach to human capabilities. If you cannot command people to love others, at least you have a better chance of having them not harm them. People know intimately, from a multitude of life-events, what it is to be wronged, mistreated, hurt. Knowing how distasteful and painful these moments can be, Hillel is saying, "At least that!" — at the very least, don't make others feel that way.

1.

It is a Mitzvah for everyone to love every single Jew
as much as he or she loves himself or herself,
as the verse states,
"And you shall love others as you love yourself." (Leviticus 19:18)

Therefore, one must speak in praise of others,
and be careful about the other person's money and possessions
just as he or she is careful about
his or her own money and possessions
and wants his or her own dignity preserved.

One who gains status by the demeaning of someone else
has no place in the Next World.

(Maimonides, Mishnah Torah,
De'ot 6:4)

2.

Positive Mitzvah #206:

This is the commandment that we were commanded
to love each other just as we love ourselves.

That is to say
that my concern and love for other Jews
should be the same as my concern and love for myself —
as far as both possessions and personal needs are involved —
for whatever the other person's possessions and wishes.

Whatever I want for myself,
I want the same for that other person.

And whatever I do not want for myself or my friends,
I do not want for that other person.

This is the meaning of the verse,
"And you shall love the other person as yourself." (Leviticus 19:18)

(Maimonides, Sefer HaMitzvot)

"Love others as you would love yourself" is a very general principle and
possibly so vague as to be abused, Maimonides becomes very specific.

Text #1:

A. Loving other Jews is a Mitzvah like any other Mitzvah, and, therefore, just as we are to keep the Shabbat, not steal, honor parents, so, too, we are to practice this Mitzvah of love.

B. "speak in praise of others": a conscious, positive act, not only looking for the good qualities of others, but also verbalizing their good points.

C. "money and possessions": very down-to-earth. The haziness of "Love others as you would love yourself" is tied very much to how we treat the common possessions of others. We don't want people stealing from us or abusing what we have. In turn, we should not steal the things others own, nor abuse what they have.

D. "gains status by demeaning": stepping over or stepping on others is prohibited by this Mitzvah. It still stuns me, as a Jewish educator, that — despite the many examples of honest, decent business people — that students of all ages insist that "it is the way of the business world" to climb over people to get where you have to get to get ahead.

Text #2:

A. "whatever I want for myself": succinctly and eloquently stated. If I wish to have peace of mind, security, a decent living, friends, family, good health for myself, I am to wish that for others also, and to act in such a way as to allow others to have those blessings.

B. "whatever I do not want for myself": as I would not want to suffer hunger, homelessness, joblessness, ill health and disease, personal tragedies of every kind, so, too, I would not wish that on others. And I would have to act to prevent these misfortunes happening to them.

To summarize: it is not only the *content* of Maimonides' statements that are so important, it is the *very fact* that he has made them so specific that allows us to see that Judaism takes this Mitzvah of loving others as most serious, and most practical in everyday life. This is not to imply that our teachers were not aware of the enormous difficulty in performing this Mitzvah. They were not naive.

1.
"Love others" (Leviticus 19:18) —
Because you have loved the other person,
that person will be like you.

(Kalla Rabbati 4)

2.
Any love which depends on a specific thing,
when that thing is removed, that love is finished.

But love which is not dependent on any specific thing
never ends.

(Pirke Avot 5:18)

3.
What are human beings that You are mindful of them,
mortals, that you have taken note of them?

You have made them little less than divine,
adorning them with Kavod-glory and majesty.

(Psalms 8:6)

4.
Rabbi Yehoshua ben Levi said:

An entourage of angels always walks in front of people,
with messengers calling out.

And what do they say?
"Make way for the image of the Holy One!"

(Deuteronomy Rabba, Re'eh 4)

Text #1 is powerful, and at the first glance, confusing. By a mere twist of grammar, the so-well-known verse "Love others as you love yourself" takes on a cause-and-effect meaning: loving others will cause others to want to be like you, i.e. loving others in turn. Just exactly how true that is in the "real world" is uncertain, but even if it were true in only a limited number of human situations, it would at least alleviate many tense — even unbearable — situations. Even if this is only a "partial universal", an accumulation of small peacemakings is no small thing.

Text #2 is a reminder that the love we are speaking of has no ulterior purpose. It is pure love, simple (in the most positive sense of the term, equal to the Hebrew term "Tamim") love. The text does not speak of a love that seeks to dominate, or love-for-personal-gain. Those kinds of love are doomed. As a parent loves a child for himself or herself, so, too, love of others should be because they are human beings.

The third text spells out why people-as-people are entitled to this love: people are born glorious, nearly divine, majestic. Along the way in Life, acquired distasteful traits (obnoxiousness for one) do not remove that essential majesty and glory from the person. These negative qualities are merely an overlayer encrusting the grandeur. But the grandeur is still there, somewhere underneath.

The fourth passage is a graphic reminder, an image meant to help people remember each person's worth. The text says that, if we would only picture these angels and listen to what they are saying, then — when we encounter others — we will know how to act appropriately. It is also a reminder to ourselves that we have such angels walking in front of us. This particular text is one of the most powerful tools for teaching self-image (=God's Image) that I have discovered in Rabbinic Literature.

Idealistic, high-sounding, perhaps too high-sounding. And yet, while Tzaddikim — The Righteous Ones — may master these principles and exemplify them, the "regular people" still benefit from holding these ideals and striving to actualize them whenever the situation demands calling them to mind. If the texts provide even a few moments of relief in human relations, if they prevent even some small number of degrading moments, they will have served their purpose.

The Rabbis have taught:
Five things were said about garlic
. . . .
And there are those who say
it brings in love and drives out jealousy.

                                        (Bava Kamma 82a)

The simplest solution to the many human problems: garlic.
If word gets out, garlic futures will soar on the world markets!

Rabbi Meir said in addition [to his previous statements]:

We assist in releasing someone from a vow
by making reference to the Torah itself, saying,

"If you had known [when you said
'That person shall have no benefit from me']
that you were transgressing the Mitzvah of

'You shall not take vengeance
or bear a grudge against another' (Leviticus 19:18)

and 'You shall not hate other people in your heart' (Leviticus 19:17)

and 'You shall love others as you love yourself' (Leviticus 19:18)

and 'Let the other person live by your side
as your kinsman' (Leviticus 25:36) —
he might become poor,
and you would thereby be prevented from providing for him —

if you had known all this,
[would you have still taken the vow?]"

If the person says,
"Had I taken all of this into consideration,
I would not have made the vow" —
then he is released from his vow.

(Mishna Nedarim 9:4)

This text — particularly in translation — is a little complex. Nevertheless, in essence, it says that, when someone takes a vow that another person should not benefit from him, there are many grave consequences. Let us assume someone is so angry at another person that he or she says, "I want nothing to do Mr. Ploni, and I want him to have nothing to do with me." If, later on, the person regrets having taken the vow, what can be done to alleviate the situation?

The Rabbinic procedure is to go either to a Sage or to three "regular" people (who constitute a legal court), to explain the situation, and to see if they might not be able to find a "Petach" — a doorway, some exit from the obligation. The Talmud discusses many doorways, often bringing to light circumstances the person taking the vow may not have considered when he took the vow.

In this case, the Sage or the court-of-three ask the person who took the vow if he had considered the fact that he was transgressing a number of Mitzvot by having taken this vow, specifically: (1) Not taking vengeance, (2) Not bearing a grudge, (3) Loving others, and (4) Performing the Mitzvah of Tzedakah. If the person who took the vow then realizes how serious was this act of driving human beings apart, rather than drawing them together, then they may release him from the vow.

This is a prime example of how seemingly abstract ideals are brought into play in the realm of Halacha-Jewish law. The ostensibly lofty principles are brought very much down to earth.

KLAL YISRAEL — ALL JEWS

I. Definition

Klal Yisrael means all Jews — everyone: Jewish prisoners, IQ-deficient Jews, Jews with an extra chromosome who languish in non-Jewish homes because no Jews will take them in, battered Jews, Jews who are old-time Yiddish-speaking Socialists, alcoholic Jews and Jewish drug abusers, rich and poor Jews and middle-income Jews, Orthodox Jews, simple and fancy-schmancy Jews, downtrodden and lonely Jews, the burned Jews and the scarred Jews (by accident or by defense of the Homeland), the deformed Jews and ugly Jews as well as the gorgeous ones, Jews with AIDS and nowhere to go in some Jewish communities, elderly Jews (Moses told Pharaoh that they would leave Egypt with old and young alike), Reform Jews, hungry Jews and poor Jews — the ones who cannot afford a decent Passover or Purim, or any Passover or Purim at all, or have no family in the whole world to eat Shabbas dinner with, Reconstructionist Jews, homeless Jews, unemployed Jews, displaced Jews, suicidal Jews, imglicklich Jews, i.e., Jews who have never had any luck in life, sad Jews, momzerish-and-arrogant Jews, humble-and-decent Jews, Conservative Jews, caring and callous Jews, Jews who are hot shots and Jews who are shleppers, crooked and honest Jews, Soviet Jews who would be free and who would be free and involved and Soviet Jews who would be free and uninvolved, Jews living in terror and Jews unaware of the blessings of life, liberty, and the pursuit of happiness or unable to attain those blessings, Jews who used to be non-Jews, insightful and dull and boring Jews, scholarly and ignorant Jews, wise and foolish Jews, active and committed and assimilated Jews, Jews who are hypocrites and Jews who are sincere, insensitive Jews, and those who can't sleep at night for the suffering of Klal Yisrael.

And that is just some small portion of the Jewish People.

And as my friend, Mark Stadler, has pointed out to me, when the Torah states that God spoke to all the children of Israel, it means all of them.

II. The Individual Jew's Relationship to Klal Yisrael

There are many reasons for the individual Jew to tie himself or herself intimately to the rest of the Jewish people. Each one, some of them together, or all of these reasons could well justify a sense of Kavod-dignity (and respect) and Ahava-love for all other Jews, and a vigorous attempt at Hava'at Shalom-Making Peace. These are just a few of those reasons —

The "existential" reason (for Jews who were born Jewish): Just being born into a certain group carries a certain mystery.... "Why, throughout all the ages, throughout the history of human beings from the very beginning of humanity was I born in such-and-such a place at such-and-such a time as part of this particular group of people?" In search of that meaning, that element which is by dint of birth "my own", I discover more about myself as a person and where I fit into the greater scheme of things. For those who have chosen the Jewish people by means of the process of conversion, reasons for involvement are somewhat easier because an active choice was made to be a part of this group. Judaism was not thrust upon them automatically by the event of birth.

The "anti-loneliness" reason: Over and against the chill of a potentially neutral, amorphous, and/or threatening world, belonging-in-and-of-itself provides comfort, warmth, and peace of mind. "This is my group, after all. They are mine, and I am theirs."

The "Image of God" reason: All human beings are similar, but I can understand my humanness more fully and more easily by living my life through the specific character of this particular group. "I can better understand the meaning of the flow of history through understanding the flow of Jewish history, I can better grasp the nature of human interaction by grasping how Jews interact with each other and with other groups of people, and I can sense the relationship of God to people more fully if I examine the relationship of God with the Jewish people."

The "right-and-decent thing to do" reason: Turning one's back on family and extended family is unfair, a denial of responsibility. "I wouldn't want people to abandon me. I shouldn't do that to others, to My People."

The "shared fate" reason: The long history of the Jews, with all its high points and sufferings is an all-pervading presence in the life of the Jew. In particular, the Shoah (English translation, though not equivalent term: Holocaust) most starkly of all raises questions and more questions and brings to the Jew's attention mysteries and more mysteries which cannot be avoided. Michel Goldberg, in his book, Namesake (Corgi Books, 1984), speaks of his definition of a Jew. Goldberg's father was murdered by the Nazis, and he describes his definition as being "circumstantial, malodorous." He states it starkly, baldly, "Whoever has gone or would have gone to the oven is a Jew." For Goldberg, there was only one differentiation between types of Jews — some produced white smoke (from having been in the camp for a long time), and others produced dark smoke "...for the newcomers, who still had a little fat on their bones."

Once, when there was a drought [in Eretz Yisrael],
Rabbi Yehuda HaNassi opened the food warehouses
and announced,

"Let all those who have studied
Bible, Mishna, Gemara, Halacha, and Aggada come in,
but those who are ignorant of Torah should not enter."

Rabbi Yonatan ben Amram forced himself in
[without identifying himself]
and said to him,
"My teacher, feed me!"

He said to him,
"My son,
have you studied the Bible?"

He answered,
"No."

"Did you study the Mishna?"

He answered,
"No."

"If that is the case, how can I feed you?"

He answered,
"Feed me as you would feed a dog or a raven."

He fed him.

When [Rabbi Yonatan ben Amram] left,
Rabbi Yehuda HaNassi remained troubled, saying,
"Woe is me!
I have given food to one who is ignorant of Torah."

His son, Rabbi Shimon said,
"Maybe that was your student, Rabbi Yonatan ben Amram,
who has never wanted to gain any advantage
because he has studied Torah?"

They checked and discovered that that was, indeed, the case.

**Rabbi Yehuda HaNassi then said,
"Let everyone enter."**

(Bava Batra 8a)

This tale is 1800 years old.

It is such a troubling story.

It could have been edited out of the Talmud because of its harshness, but it wasn't, and the fact that it remains in our literature must mean it was left there to instruct us. The opening lines make no sense to me: how can Rabbi Yehuda HaNassi, leader of the Jews in Palestine, deny food to starving people simply on the basis of their Torah education? What of the Jews who were so poor they had to work day in and day out to eke out a living, returning home too exhausted to study? What of the Jews whose minds were limited, unable to grasp the more sophisticated intricacies of Torah study? What of those who showed no interest in Torah study and who were as hungry as anyone else, who felt the pain and suffering of having no food to eat?

I admit that the story *does* have a comforting solution. But as Elie Wiesel has taught over and over again, the questions are much more significant than the answers and solutions. And these questions do not easily go away just because one of Rabbi Yehuda HaNassi's students forced the crisis to some more humane resolution.

Is the point that — in the face of outrageous injustice and enormous human suffering — we are to use all manner of radical methods to alleviate human suffering?

Is the point that — in the face of hunger and the bloated stomachs of children unfed for days and no hope for even minimal recovery — is the point that lesser scholars and less famous Jews are the real teachers of the Great?

Are we to derive from this text that we have been studying Torah all wrong, that while every Talmud student knows the name of Rabbi Yehuda HaNassi — compiler and editor of the Mishna — the name we should *really* know is that of Rabbi Yonatan ben Amram?

Are we to study this text, and — even should we forget some of the details — are we to forever remember how shocked we were, or if we were not shocked, how stunned we ought to have been at what transpired centuries ago in the face of catastrophe in the Holy Land? Is this tale to become in our minds like the memory of a bad dream whose contents we have forgotten, but still we recall how profoundly troubling the dream had been?

It is such a troubling and vital story for our times.

HAVA'AT SHALOM — PEACEMAKING

Now, how do we do it?

Practically speaking, how do we set about making these mitzvahs of Providing Dignity-Kavod, Love of Jews-Ahavat Yisrael, and most of all Bringing Peace-Hava' at Shalom Bayn Adam LeChavayro a reality?

1. Use all methods, all materials, all quirks and twists of talents we can: curricula and texts and 3 X 5's and sourcebooks and courses and roleplayings, plays, concerts, art exhibits, toys, dolls, coupons, fairs and circuses, videos, games and posters, T-shirts and trading cards, retreats, organizations, money, Halachot and Aggadot, seminars, stories told by sublime storytellers, kiddies' books, neologisms, metaphors, similes and analogies and poetic soarings, teach-ins, coalition builders, conflict resolvers, prejudice reducers, arbiters, conciliators, negotiators, heroes and out-of-the-way people, competents and crazies and clear-thinking philosophers and theologians, mentors, and Peaceloving Rebbis, perspectivizers, personality changers, beggings and pleas, psychologists, MSW's, experts, technicians, heroes and peacepipes— whatever we have in our resources, anything, everything....We must keep peacemaking on the agenda, at all costs, at all inconveniences if necessary. E.g.:

2. E.g., conferences and seminars and sit-downs with coffee and muffins.

3. E.g., working with groups like the National Coalition Building Institute, a dynamic group in Massachusetts that goes anywhere and everywhere (Northern Ireland, for example) to bring about reconciliation and peace. And the AAA: the American Arbitration Association.

4. E.g., educators teaching it, so that we will raise up a generation (including ourselves) of Mevi' ay Shalom-Peacemakers. It is much easier for us to find Tzedakah Heroes, and to train Tzedakah heroes, than it is to find or train Mevi' ay Shalom. And that's a fact. We need more experts and actualizers in the glorious field of Hava' at Shalom Bayn Adam LeChavayro.

5. E.g., marriage and divorce counsellors and those who work with battered spouses (battered and battering) know things we don't know. We should call on them to teach us. Sadly, there may be too solid an analogy there between domestic violence and violence in the Jewish community.

6. E.g., We should make a point of associating with Peacemakers, of becoming their students and followers. We should make our friends and companions and acquaintances those who believe in Peacemaking, people in whose presence and away from whom we would be embarrassed to be vicious, meanspirited, peacebreakers. People of stature. I cannot stress enough how much we should seek out these individuals and make them a part of our lives. We should become not only Ohavay Shalom-Lovers of Peace but also Rodefay Shalom, running everywhere to make peace. (Shalom is one of God's names, and one of the names of the Mashiach according to the Talmud.) Groups can form called Chevrot Mevi' ay

Shalom devoting themselves to this particular all-important Mitzvah, learning about it, but, more important, actively making peace.

   It's the right thing to do.

1.
When our love was strong,
we could have slept on the broad side of a sword.

Now that our love is no longer strong,
a bed 60 cubits wide is not big enough for us.

(Sanhedrin 7a)

2.
It is easy to acquire an enemy
and difficult to acquire a friend.

(Yalkut Shimoni,
Va'Etchanan 845)

3.
Ben Azzai says:

...Who is the strongest of the strong?
One who overcomes one's inclinations-to-do-harm.

There are those who say:
One who turns an enemy into a friend.

(Avot DeRabbi Natan 23)

The first text provides a not-easily-forgotten image about love, expressed with a touch of humor.

In the good days, there was great intimacy, but things have been so bad, 60 cubits (=about 90 feet) isn't enough bed space.

This same sigh of recollection of better times applies to all kinds of interpersonal relations, not just intimacy of spouses. The pain of alienation from others is that much stronger when the partners, the friends, the associates remember how good it was when their relationship worked better.

Recalling the heady days in 1948 when the State of Israel was being born, or the high times following the Six Day War or after the Entebbe Rescue in 1976, when there was such closeness among the people, we ought to strive to re-achieve those feelings of common goals and needs, the sheer joy of the feelings of oneness.

The second text carries a great burden and a warning: solid, true friends are hard to come by. We should value them, treat them well, preserve the uniqueness and wondrousness of the relationship. So many things can go wrong and the circumstances of life are such that any one of a vast number of happenings can ruin things. Friends become enemies, and the pain is compounded. Not only that, but acquaintances become enemies, and strangers become enemies.

It is a commonplace to say that at many times throughout history the Jewish People have had few friends. If strains develop in the relationships among Jews, we should recall how much we ought to value and work at preserving our friendships among ourselves.

The third passage makes clear that peacemaking is no easy task, particularly if you are one of the parties and not merely the arbiter. What strength is involved? Overcoming prejudices, the strength to be humble, to admit personal shortcomings, to see the justice in the other party's position, to surrender certain points without surrendering personal integrity, to face the other party squarely, to face oneself honestly. Formidable tasks, formidable demands, formidable strength.

1.
It was taught —

Rabbi Tarfon said:

**I would be surprised if there were anyone in this generation
who knows how to take criticism.**

**If someone says,
"Take the toothpick from between your teeth,"
the other person replies,
"First take the board out from between your eyes."**

(Arachin 16b)

2.
Rabbi Elazar ben Azariah said:

**I would be surprised if there were anyone in this generation
who knows how to criticize.**

[Rashi: "Who knows how to criticize" —
Respectfully, without the other's face changing color from humiliation.]

(Arachin 16b)

3.
Rabbi Yishmael the son of Rabbi Yossi says:
. . . .
**Do not say, "You have to accept my opinion!" —
It is their prerogative, not yours.**

(Pirke Avot 4:10)

Again and again it needs to be stated: Rabbinic texts are not naive. The Rabbis did not live in some rarified scholarly atmosphere away from people and their daily activities. They were obsessed with and extraordinarily keen observers of human interrelationships. They knew, as we know, that people don't like to take criticism. Text #1 takes this further: the grotesque image of "the board...from between your eyes" shows how far people will go to lash out in the face of criticism (constructive or otherwise).

Rabbi Elazar ben Azariah rounds out the picture: criticizing takes sensitivity and a sense of respect for the one being criticized. Criticism is more an art than a science; it takes all kinds of skills and creativity that can't be defined by hard-and-fast rules. There are no simple handbooks that say, "In situation A, criticize this way. In Situation B, do as follows."

Rabbi Yishmael the son of Rabbi Yossi's statement is an antidote to pushiness. Opinionated people try to thrust their ideas on others (a violation of their Kavod-Dignity). The art of it all is offering the opinion and leaving the other to judge its value.

These texts bring us very much back into the Real World. But underlying the three statements is the question, "Just what exactly is Human Nature?" Do we accept that "that's just the way people are (ourselves included)"? Or do we put up the good fight to counteract these tendencies?

1.
Rabbi Natan says:

Don't taunt others with your own shortcomings.

(Bava Metzia 59b)

2.
Fix up your own looks
and only afterwards see how others look.

[=Make sure of your own character
before you go picking away at others.]

(Sanhedrin 18a)

3.
Chizkia said in the name of Rabbi Yirmia
who said in the name of Rabbi Shimon bar Yochai,

"I have seen those who are in the Upper Reaches [of Paradise],
and they are very few in number."

(Sanhedrin 97b)

The first two texts are meant as practical peacemaking techniques: conflict and confrontation can be eased — sometimes — if we call to mind our own flaws. If we would do that when we are about to tear away at someone else, we might reconsider our course of action. After scanning a few modern day rabbis' views on the subject (e.g., Rabbi Yitzchak Magrisso in the *Me'Am Lo'ez*, Rabbi Yehuda Gershuni's *Kol Tzofyich*, where besides stating his own opinions, he also quotes Rav Kook), I discovered one abundantly clear position: before taking the step of criticizing the others, we should double-check to see if we have our Tzaddik certificates on the wall.

The third text is a favorite of mine: Rabbi Shimon bar Yochai reminds us that those that deserve the title of "Tzaddik First Class" are *very* few, indeed.

1.
Conflict is like a water pipe with a hole in it —
once the water begins to seep through,
the hole gets larger and the water gushes out.

Abaye the Elder said:

It is like a plank in a footbridge —
once the plank begins to settle,
it becomes that much more firmly fixed.

(Sanhedrin 7a)

2.
Rav Huna said:

It is written,
"You shall not take vengeance or bear a grudge
against others of your people". (Leviticus 19:18)

What would be a good analogy in this situation?

If a person was slicing a piece of meat,
and the knife cuts his hand,
should that person then turn around
and cut the hand that had caused the injury?

(Jerusalem Talmud,
Nedarim 9:4)

3.
If a poor person asks for Tzedakah from you
and you do not have the means to assist,
speak to the poor person in a soothing manner.

It is prohibited to be nasty to the poor person
or to shout at him
because his heart is broken and crushed.
. . . .
As the verse states,
"[God]...
revives the spirits of those who are low,
and revives the hearts of the crushed." (Isaiah 57:15)

Woe to the person who humiliates the poor person!
Woe to him!

Rather, one should react to that person as a parent would,
both as far as feelings of caring are concerned
and as far as the manner of speaking are concerned.

(Maimonides, Mishna Torah,
Laws of Gifts to the Poor, 10:5)

4.
Rabbi Yehoshua says:

Stinginess,
the inclination-to-do-harm,
and hatred of other human beings
destroy a person's life.

(Pirke Avot 2:16)

The Talmud uses many tools and methods in its attempt to bring the message of Shalom into the Jews' active consciousness. Stories of Peacemakers like Aaron (explained further on) are one way to convey the message. Halachot-laws are another approach. Analogies, metaphors, similes and other literary devices are also summoned by the Rabbis in this difficult quest for peace.

Text #1 employs two simple and eminently sensible images: the leaking pipe and the planks of a bridge. On the other hand, pace is like putting on a new jacket or pair of pants: when you first put them on, they may be a little tight, but then the threads of the material begin to "settle", and the fit becomes more comfortable.

Text #2 is, I believe, a much more striking image: one hand causes pain to the other. Does it make any sense, therefore, to multiply the pain and doubly cripple the body? It is much stronger stuff than "Two wrongs don't make a right" or "Don't lower yourself to their level" and similar phrases. Anyone who has cut his or her hand while preparing food recalls the surprise-and-shock, the pain, the blood, the fear that the damage is irreparable. And yet, with all that, we would never think to take the knife and turn it on the "offending hand", multiplying the shock, the pain, the blood. Why then, the Talmud teaches, would we want to do that with other human beings?

Educators could supplement the list of analogies, metaphors, comparisons, and logical and associative techniques to help people focus on their sense of Ahava, Kavod, and Shalom...love, dignity, and peace.

E.g., do we love our pets more than we love other Jews or human beings?

E.g., do we love other Jews and human beings as much as we love a good cup of coffee in the morning that wakes us up and gets our mind buzzing and flying?

E.g., do we love and care for, and speak in praise of, other Jews and human beings as much as our new car? Do we lovingly describe every detail and feature that brings us pleasure, and make moderate (or even silly) excuses to explain away the shortcomings of other Jews and human beings as we do when we say, "Well, it does take a while to get the new Thunderbird warmed up in the morning, and it doesn't corner quite the way I like it....But it's a terrific car anyway!'"?

E.g., do we love other Jews and human beings as much as, or in the same way as, we love friends, spouses, one's own children? And, do we do things for other Jews and human beings the same way, and to the same extent, as for friends, spouses, children, pets?

E.g., do we love strangers more (and understandably so sometimes) than those closer to us by blood relation or destiny?

And finally, e.g., so many of us were taught to pick up a holy book and kiss it if it falls to the ground — does it not make logical sense that the same must be done for other Jews and human beings who have fallen to the ground? Books have no feelings, no sense of pain and loneliness; people suffer. We are quick to respond to the book, slower with people. It is illogical, and if we were the one who had fallen, would we not be hurt and offended that others were more meticulous about a book than about us? Text #3 offers an eloquent insight into such an encounter with other people. And what is most striking is, even though the passage is from a law code, Maimonides — rather than be dispassionate because he is describing the law — writes very emphatically, "Woe to him!"...And he repeats the phrase "Woe to him!" The situation of "haves" and "have-nots" is so potentially explosive, we are reminded to be aware of what we have in common, not what divides us. What we have in common is our common "human beingness", whereas what divides the Tzedakah-giver from the recipient is only a matter of money.

The fourth passage is neither an analogy nor a rhetorical device. It is, rather, a simple, bald, and powerful statement that certain things eat up our lives, not the least of which is hatred of others. We know it's true; we read it in the newspapers every day, hear it on the news on the hour, view it in a multitude of common human situations. Therapists will tell us that — at the very least — discovering and admitting that there *is* a problem is the first step towards a solution.

1.
You shall not hate others in your heart.

(Leviticus 19:17)

2.
Negative Mitzvah #302:

This is the warning we were given
not to hate one another,
as the verse states,
"You shall not hate others in your heart". (Leviticus 19:17)

The language of the [Midrash collection] Sifra is:
I [God] am speaking here of hate in the heart.

However, if the person reveals his hate to the other,
and that other one becomes aware of the fact that he hates him,
the person does not transgress this negative Mitzvah.

But he *does* transgress
"You shall not take vengeance
or bear a grudge against another" (Leviticus 19:17)
and also transgresses the positive commandment which states,
"Love others as you love yourself". (Leviticus 19:18)

Hate in the heart is the most serious transgression of all.

(Maimonides, Sefer HaMitzvot)

3.
....
In any event,
hate in the heart is tougher than any open hate....

Any intelligent person can see that
this is the lowest and ugliest human trait of all.

(Sefer HaChinuch, 248)

During the course of Jewish history, a number of attempts were made to number the 613 Mitzvot and to expand on the source-references in the Torah. *Sefer HaMitzvot* by Maimonides (1135-1204) is one such attempt, divided into Positive Mitzvot (248 of them), and Negative Mitzvot (365). The *Sefer HaChinuch* (end of the 13th Century) is another, enumerating the Mitzvot according to the order of their appearance in the Torah.

The specific emphasis of this Mitzvah is that, if the source of the hate can be brought out into the open, at least there is some hope of reconciliation, relief, and reparation.

1.
Rabbi Yochanan HaSandlar teaches,

"Every gathering which is for the sake of Heaven
will stand the test of time.

But every gathering which is not for the sake of Heaven
will not stand the test of time."

(Pirke Avot 4:14)

2.
[At the time of Creation]
only one person was created
in order to teach us...that
— for the sake of peace —
no one should say to another person,
"My ancestor was greater than your ancestor."
. . .
And in order to emphasize the greatness of the Holy One:

When human beings mint coins,
they make many coins from one die,
and they are all alike.

But the King of kings of kings,
the Holy One, blessed be He,
"minted" all human beings with the die of Adam,
and not a single one resembles another.

Therefore,
everyone must say,
"The whole world was created for me."

(Mishna Sanhedrin, Chapter 4, end)

If we restrict the context of this passage to conferences concerning Klal Yisrael — the Unity of the Entire Jewish People — we ought to ask why Rabbi Yochanan HaSandlar expresses such optimism?

Perhaps it is because issues-in-the-abstract no longer remain abstract, but people are face to face, and somewhere during the talk-time the differences among the parties can at least be brought into clearer focus, *once each person recognizes something of himself or herself in the other person.* Not only are we all descended from one common ancestor, Adam, but, though one face may be a little rounder, one body-shape more lean, one mind a little quicker or slower, the same die was used for all of us. It would seem, then, that all gatherings, conferences, retreats, seminars, and similar ventures bringing disparate elements within the community together — *if there is an honest desire for exchange and mutual respect* — are bound to produce some positive results.

This second passage is a fine antidote to arrogance, pontification, and self-righteousness. It is The Great Equalizer.

At a bar/bat Mitzvah ceremony for Jewish retarded adults who are residents of group homes in the area, one of the speakers pointed out that we have no description of Adam's mental capacities, no IQ comparisons, no test scores to establish intellectual achievement. Above or below the 100 mark on IQ tests is not the determining factor or criterion for measuring a person's nature or worth. We are all descendants of the first human being, and being human is the common thread.

In the Jewish context, there is an interesting note on a passage in Pirke Avot that Yom Tov Lipmann Heller (1579-1654) mentions (quoting another source unfamiliar to me) in his Tosfot Yom Tov commentary. The text in Avot says, "Rabbi Chanina ben Tradyon says, 'Two who sit together without exchanging words of Torah constitute a get-together of scorners.'" (3:2) Tosfot Yom Tov says that both are, in fact, engaged in Torah study, but both keep it to themselves, neither thinking that the other's Torah is of any value, and therefore there is no need to exchange Torah-ideas. It is an easy step from denying the value of a person's Torah-insights to denying that person's worth as a Jew.

Having taken part in an all-day seminar on Klal Yisrael where part of the program offered three prominent rabbis the opportunity to teach the audience their views of a particular Torah passage, I can see the effectiveness of such joint ventures. On the one hand, participants from less traditional backgrounds listened intently to the Orthodox Rabbi's insights, and the more traditional Jews found the Reform Rabbi's teachings of great interest. And everything in between....It is as if the "definitionness" and "labellingness" of "Orthodox", "Conservative", "Reform", "Reconstructionist", "Secular Jew" fell by the wayside as we settled in to study Torah together. While we studied Torah together, there was common ground for everyone, and Torah neutralized any other tensions at issue while we were studying.

1.
Rabbi Akiva said:

Even the poorest of poor Jews...
are descendants of Abraham, Isaac, and Jacob.

(Bava Kamma 90b)

2.
All Jews are relatives and friends.

(Tanchuma, Neso 1)

3.
Rabbi Shimon is the one who said,
"All Jews are descendants of royalty."

(Shabbat 67a)

4.
All Jews have a place in the Next World.

(Mishna Sanhedrin 11:1)

5.
All Jews are responsible for one another.

(Shevu'ot 39a)

Here are five more "equalizing" texts, reminders of what Jews have in common and what ought to hold them together.

"Even the poorest...": Economic success or failure is irrelevant. We have common ancestry.

"...Abraham, Isaac, and Jacob": Sarah, Rebecca, Rachel, and Leah. Seven grand forebears remembered for their human qualities, not their financial triumphs. While the Book of Genesis mentions that Abraham was wealthy, we remember him more, and wish to emulate him more, for his foresight, vision, and sweeping hospitality to strangers.

"...relatives and friends": For those who don't get along with their relatives, then we should remember how we relate to our friends; if we find friends in short supply, the reminder that we Jews are all relatives should reinforce in us what blood-relationships can provide as a sense of belonging and mutual assistance.

"...royalty": Should a royal personage come our way, we would treat the king or queen with a certain unique sense of respect. Rabbi Shimon reminds us that that is how we should treat all Jews (ourselves included).

"...have a place in the Next World": We should not be so quick to say who is worthy and who is unworthy.

"...responsible for one another": The Hebrew word for "responsible" is "Arayvim", which literally means a "guarantor" for a loan. As my friend and teacher, Rabbi Jonathan Porath, has pointed out to me, that means quite clearly that if the other defaults on his or her responsibility, we have to make good, because we have co-signed on the loan. In economic terms, modern Israel attaches the phrase "BeAyravon [same root as Arayv] Mugbal" after the name of a bank or a company. This is comparable to the British term "Ltd.", meaning "Limited Liability". For us as Jews, there is no "Ayravon Mugbal", no Limited Liability. What- ever compensation must be made, *we are responsible to compensate*...no limits.

1.
"Seek peace and pursue it" (Psalm 34:15) —

Seek it out locally,
and run to make peace anyplace else it might be needed.

(Avot DeRabbi Natan 12)

2.
For I have selected him [Abraham]
so that he may instruct his children
and his posterity after him
to keep God's ways:
to do what is just and right. [Tzedakah U'Mishpat]

(Genesis 18:19)

3.
David reigned over all Israel,
and David executed true justice [Mishpat U'Tzedakah]
among all his people.

(II Samuel 8:15)

4.
Blessed are You, Lord,
A King Who loves Tzedakah U'Mishpat.

(Siddur)

Peacemaking is not simply a "when-it-comes-our-way" Mitzvah, unlike Shabbat which is a once-a-week event or Yom Kippur fasting on an annual basis. Jewish tradition bids us actively seek out opportunities to make peace, locally, or at the far stretches of civilized life.

Why be a peacemaker? On the pragmatic level, peace is certainly more pleasant than war, tension, dissent, divisiveness. But there are additional, higher reasons for peacemaking:

"For I have selected him...": Abraham (and subsequently all Jews thereafter) was selected to actualize in his own life the qualities of what is Just and Right in life. Peace is Just and Right. We are Jews, descendants of Abraham. Therefore, we are to attempt to make peace happen.

"And David executed true justice...": Using the same two Hebrew words as God applies to Abraham, the Book of Samuel records that King David did exactly that — brought "Mishpat" and "Tzedakah" to reality among the people. Whatever his human failings, centuries later, we recall that the King made these values his highest priority. Throughout ancient history (and not-so-ancient history), royal power often implied tyranny, despotism, and an absolute disregard for the needs of the people. Not so with King David. He understood that the purpose of power was to bring about a just society and a decent place for all to live.

"...Who loves Tzedakah U'Mishpat": The Jewish view of *Imitatio Dei*, imitating God, is an activist approach, i.e., if *God* loves Tzedakah U'Mishpat — doing what is Just and Right, then *we*, too, should love Tzedakah U'Mishpat and play our part in making these abstract concepts real. This blessing, part of the three-times-daily prayers, is a constant reminder of our obligation as Jews to bring more Tzedakah and Mishpat into the world.

(In a lighter vein, it is interesting to note that on TV a most grandfatherly figure has been advising people to eat their Quaker oatmeal because "It's the right thing to do." How can you *not* eat your oatmeal after an appeal like that?)

1.
Hillel says:

Be among Aaron's students —
loving peace,
pursuing peace,
loving other human beings,
and bringing them close to the Torah.

(Pirke Avot 1:12)

2.
Aaron was a lover and pursuer of peace,
a peacemaker among human beings.

(Sanhedrin 6b)

In Rabbinic Literature, Aaron the High Priest is considered the paradigm of peacemakers. In these two passages we see not only that he had the reputation of a lover of peace, but also one who pursued it, going out of his way to make peace happen. Text #1 reveals the source of this obsession with peacemaking — he loved other human beings. (The Chassidic Master, Abraham Joshua Heschel, "The Apter Rebbi", requested that his epitaph read "Ohev Yisrael"—"Lover of the Jews".) It would follow naturally, then, that he would want them to live in peace. But *wanting* peace was not enough; he *acted* on his wishes instead of simply sitting back and lamenting the strife and tensions he saw among the Jews of his day.

1.
Rabbi Meir says:

What is the meaning of the verse,
"And he held many back from sin"? (Malachi 2:6)

When Aaron would be walking along
and run into a bad or wicked person,
he would greet him [Natan lo Shalom].

If, sometime in the future,
that person set out to do something wrong,
he would say,

"Woe is me!
How can I look Aaron in the eye after I do such a thing?!
I would be so embarrassed because he greeted me."

The end result was
that the person would restrain himself from wrongdoing.

Similarly,
when he would see two people arguing with each other,
Aaron would go and sit with one of them and say,

"My son,
see what your friend is saying —
he is tearing his heart out,
and ripping his clothing —
and saying,

'Woe is me!
How can I look my friend in the eye?
I am so ashamed that I have done him wrong.'"

And he would sit with that person
until he removed all the ill-will from his heart.

Then Aaron would go and sit with the other one and say,

"My son,
see what your friend is saying —
he is tearing his heart out,

and ripping his clothing —
and saying,

'Woe is me!
How can I look my friend in the eye?
I am so ashamed because I have done him wrong.'"

And he would sit with that person
until he removed all the ill-will from his heart.

Then, finally, when the two people would meet,
they would embrace and kiss each other.

(Avot DeRabbi Natan 12)

2.
Rabban Shimon ben Gamliel says:

When [Aaron] would see two people who hated each other,
he would go to Mr. X and say,

"Why do you hate Mr. Y?

He has already come to my house,
prostrated himself in front of me
and said to me,

'I have wronged Mr. Y.
Please go and placate him.'"

Then he would leave Mr. X
and go to Mr. Y
and say the same thing.

In this manner he would bring peace, and love,
and friendship between one person and another.

In this way
he brought many people back from the brink of sin.

(Perek HaShalom)

Rabbi Meir's description of Aaron gives us two illustrations of Aaron as Peacemaker, both distinct, both very instructive.

In the first situation, it is Aaron's manner which effectuated the change in the other person. Aaron would always greet people, and the fact that such an important personage did so must have impressed itself upon all those who knew him. The Hebrew phrase for "greet him" is "Natan Lo Shalom", which translates word-for-word as "Gave him peace", as if to say that this very act of saying hello was a gift, a reminder that pleasant interpersonal relations should be the common rule of daily living.

The "greetee" must have been thrown off balance: Why would so prominent a leader, so powerful a person take the trouble to greet me? He must think I am someone of importance. From that starting point, the person could analogize to others, that, he or she, too, must do the same for others, greeting them, valuing them, "giving them peace", as it were. Conversely, not doing the same for others would mean they have personally failed Aaron, a deep embarrassment for them.

In practical terms for our times, it would seem we need to discover or train those people who are or will be of such stature that we would react similarly: we would be too embarrassed to face them if we did not live up to their expectations in the realm of human relations.

In the second situation, we see Aaron in the thick of his peacemaking. Hava'at Shalom Bayn Adam LeChavayro-Peacemaking, can be *very* uncomfortable, *very* daunting. It would appear that Aaron did not hesitate to take this responsibility upon himself. He employs "every trick in the book", even stretching the truth, to bring about this all-important human reconciliation. There are so many easier Mitzvahs to perform, ones that don't tear at your guts. Making a blessing over wine or bread entails no pain. Hava'at Shalom is painful. Lighting Channukah candles is not threatening. Hava'at Shalom — Making Peace can be threatening. Planting trees in Israel can only bring joy and benefit. Hava'at Shalom can be depressing, fraught with tension, explosive.

Text #2 retells the story of Aaron's techniques using slightly different wording. I record it because the variant phrasing helps flesh out the complexity of the process and the greatness of the rewards., i.e. bringing back many from the brink of the sin of hating others.

**Why was Moses privileged to have the unique facial radiance
in this world
that is normally reserved for the Righteous Ones
in the Next World?**

**Because throughout his life he carried out God's wishes,
and agonized over the honor [Kavod] due to God
and the dignity [Kavod] the Jews deserve,
and enormously craved peace between the Jews
and their parent in Heaven.**

(Seder Eliahu Rabba 4)

Moses's Jewish obsessions were somewhat different than Aaron's, and yet not so different.

Aaron was obsessed with loving Jews; Moses concentrated on their dignity. Both qualities follow each other and lead to the other. They overlap and interplay.

Aaron used all his human powers to bring peace among Jews; Moses wanted to insure that there would be peace between Jews and God. Both issues follow each other and lead to the other. They overlap and interplay and complement each other.

1.
There were certain thugs who lived
in Rabbi Meir's neighborhood
who used to push him around a lot.

He used to pray that they should die.

His wife Beruriah said to him,

"What do you think?
Is it because a verse states,
'Let the wrongdoers disappear'? (Psalm 105:35)

That verse really says,
'Let *wrongdoing* disappear.'

Besides, look at the end of that verse,
'And wrongdoers will be no more' —
Once the *wrongdoing* disappears,
then there will be no more wrongdoers.

What you should be doing is praying
that they should change their ways,
and then they will not be wrongdoers."

He then prayed on their behalf,
and they changed their ways.

(Berachot 10a)

2.
There were two men —
provoked by Satan —
who used to fight with each other every Friday evening.

Rabbi Meir once came to where they were.

He stopped them from quarreling for three Friday evenings
until he finally made peace between them.

He heard [Satan] say,
"Woe is me!
Rabbi Meir has driven me from this house."

(Gittin 52a)

In the First Century, Rabbi Meir is described in terms very similar to those applied to Aaron the Peacemaker.

The first text — a little complex in translation — boils down to the fact that Rabbi Meir condemned the bullies instead of condemning their deeds. Beruriah, his wife, indicated that he was taking the wrong approach: *the act* is what we should hate, not *the person.*.

That makes sense. For sure it is reasonable, but at the same time apparently humanly impossible in so many human situations where human cruelty abounds. Let us split the reaction to two levels: for Saintly People, Beruriah's principle should be considered absolute. (In Jewish life a number of names come to mind, not the least of which is the late Reb Aryeh Levine, known as the Jerusalem Tzaddik. In secular life, Lehavdil, one recalls lines like Boys Town's Father Flanagan's, "There's no such thing as a bad kid.") But for the others, we, the "regular folk", we should not shy from applying Beruriah's Rule to as many situations as possible. If it works in Real Life only 10% of the time or 14% of the time or 8.3% of the time, the benefits are still enormous.

The Denver Post (December 16, 1988) describes a certain 6-foot-5 Leon Kelly who is working miracles with gangs in that city. He is a former cocaine dealer, a near-suicide, and a man who knows the consequences of such a lifestyle, having served three years in the Colorado prison in Cañon City. The description of Mr. Kelly is most admirable, and the reader might say to himself or herself, "unbelievable!" But that is just the point: it is not unbelievable. It is happening in some places, and these courageous Peace Maestros should become the real instructors for others who would wish to take part in such Mitzvah work. Don't misunderstand. He is not trying to make peace among the gangs....He is trying to get the whole idea of Ganghood out of the consciousness of the youth of Denver. And, apparently, he is succeeding to some degree.

The second text sounds very much like the texts about Aaron I mentioned previously. The added element is Satan's lament. In the Talmud, Satan is mythical personification of the troublemaker, the cause of dissension and enmity. It is a fine image the Talmud describes — that even the Arch-Momzer has to admit defeat in the presence of the likes of a Rabbi Meir.

There is another, stranger, case involving Rabbi Meir's peacemaking efforts (Jerusalem Talmud, Sotah 1:4), where he allows someone's wife to publicly spit in his eye. It is a complicated story, but it involved husband/wife relations, high tensions, anger and jealousy, and radical action was needed to preserve peace in the household. Even though Rabbi Meir's students felt that he was debasing himself, he explained how absolutely important peace was, and how far you have to go sometimes to preserve or make peace.

Rabbi Broka Choza'a was frequently to be found
in the marketplace of Bay Lefet.

Elijah was often there with him.

Rabbi Broka asked Elijah,
"Is there anyone in the market who deserves
to receive the rewards of the Next World?"
. . . .
In the meantime,
two people came by,
and Elijah said to him,
"These will receive the rewards of the Next World."

Rabbi Broka asked them,
"What do you do?"

They replied,
"We are jokers, making sad people laugh.

Also, when we see two people arguing,
we work hard to make peace between them."

(Ta'anit 22a)

This is a curious text that is meant to catch us by surprise. If we were to circulate a questionnaire to 1,000 people by random sample, employing all the modern methods of poll-taking, a one-question questionnaire asking simply, "Who deserves the Blessings of Eternity?" — I would doubt anyone would answer, "The jokers" or "The clowns".

Assuming that we would want to employ every human talent available to bring more peace into the world, it now becomes obvious that humor would be one of the most useful tools possible.

It is most fitting to recall Sam Levenson's Grandeur of the Soul as he addressed audiences everywhere, speaking of Yiddishkeit, a good Judaism, a pleasant Jewishness, a delightful thing, this Being Jewish. Those who knew him or heard him speak only once know the good feelings, the authentic insights he had into being Jewish, and the warm feelings that came from every encounter with the man.

Returning to the text: Rabbi Broka Choza'a, Elijah, and the jokers (some texts indicate that the jokers were brothers) become much more vivid if we close our eyes and picture the scene...a crowded marketplace, people rushing here and there to buy their goods, Rabbi Broka Choza'a's look of anticipation as he scans the masses of people, and — finally — his look of surprise when he realizes just who these two people are. A wonderful Talmudic story.

1.
When the members of his community
wanted to appoint Rabbi Akiva their leader,
he said,

"Let me discuss it with my household."

They followed him
and overheard them say,

"If you take the position,
know that they will curse you and despise you."

(Jerusalem Talmud,
Pe'ah 8:6)

2.
Even though Rabbi Elazar ben Azariah assumed a position
of distinguished leadership in the community —
nevertheless, he lived a long life.

(Jerusalem Talmud,
Berachot 1:6)

The first text is a very sobering one: even the highly-respected Rabbi Akiva could not be expected to be immune from the often-nasty realities of community leadership. Politics, infighting, personality clashes would be inevitable, and painful. It takes great courage to step into a position of power, and the personal price to be paid is very high.

The second text is meant, I believe, a little humorously. The tensions of community office can be draining, even life-shortening. Rabbi Elazar ben Azariah was the exception, though we are not told the secret of his success.

1.
Why was the First Temple destroyed?

Because of three things:
idolatry, immorality, and bloodshed....

But the Second Temple
— when they were so occupied with
Torah and acts of lovingkindness —
why was it destroyed?

Because of senseless hatred [Sinat Chinnam].

(Yoma 9b)

Jerusalem was destroyed because of Kamtza and Bar Kamtza:

Once there was a man who had a friend named Kamtza
and an enemy named Bar Kamtza.

He made a banquet and said to his servant,
"Go bring Kamtza."

He went and brought Bar Kamtza.

When the host discovered Bar Kamtza sitting there,
he said to him,
"Since you are my enemy,
what are you doing here?
Get up and leave!"

He said to the host,
"Since I am already here,
let me be,
and I will pay for whatever I eat or drink."

The host said to him,
"No."

He said to the host,
"I will give you half the cost of your banquet."

The host said,
"No."

"I will pay for the entire banquet."

The host said,
"No",
grabbed him,
picked him up,
and threw him out.

Bar Kamtza said,
"Since all the Rabbis were sitting there
and didn't stop him,
I understand that they agree with what he did to me.
I will go and inform against them to the Roman Government."

He went and told Caesar,
"The Jews are revolting against you."
. . . .
It was taught:

Rabbi Elazar said,
"See how terribly great is the power of humiliation,
for God took up Bar Kamtza's cause,
ultimately destroying His own House
and burning His own Temple."

(Gittin 55b-57a)

The first text explains in general terms the well-known comparison between the reasons for both Temples being destroyed. It is stated in such a way that those who read it or hear it would say, "The reasons for the First Temple make sense. These are grave offenses." With the Second Temple, though, it is more difficult to picture what the teacher had in mind.

Text #2 is how the Talmudic Rabbis relate the sad tale of the moral degeneracy of the Jewish people just prior to 70 C.E. In literary terms they tell a story of two people, a host and a guest, and what evolved from a simple dinner invitation: the insult, the silent assent of the rabbis, the anger and turning-for-revenge to the Romans.

In the text in Gittin, between the line "The Jewish are revolting against you" and "It was taught..." there is an extremely lengthy description of how one thing led to another and to the next thing until ultimately Jerusalem and The Temple lay in ruins.

The historical facts that have been uncovered for this period describe Jew fighting Jew, factions and civil strife, a self-destructiveness that made it relatively easy for the Romans to conquer the people and the land. The Talmud simply re-tells history in its own terms.

1.
"Its [the Torah's] ways are pleasant ways,
and all its paths are peace" (Proverbs 3:17) —

Everything written in the Torah is for the sake of peace.
(Tanchuma, Tzav, Buber Edition, 5)

2.
Rabbi Yehoshua ben Levi said:
. . . .
If you have a headache, occupy yourself with Torah.
. . . .
If your entire body is in pain, occupy yourself with Torah.
(Eruvin 54a)

3.
Rav said:
The Mitzvot were given in order to tie God's creatures together.
(Yalkut Shimoni, Shemini 535)

4.
The end result of Tzedakah will be peace,
and the Tzedakah work will yield eternal peace-of-mind and security.
(Isaiah 32:17)

Torah and Mitzvot are ever-recurring themes in Rabbinic Literature.

Torah was understood by the Rabbis to be the main guide into the array of Mitzvot. The one follows the other.

Therefore, according to the above texts:

Torah should lead to peace.

Mitzvot should lead to unity.

Therefore, logically speaking:

Torah-and-Mitzvot should lead to peace-and-unity.

Therefore, even, Torah is good for headaches and body aches, when the entire people's head and body aches for whatever reason.

In an ideal world.

A variant of text #3 reads: The Mitzvot were given in order to refine human beings. (Leviticus Rabba 13:3, Margoliot 2:277) Using this reading, Mitzvot refine out jealousy, meanness, prejudice, hatred, self-centeredness, melancholy, despair, divisiveness and leave behind human qualities such as love, caring, joy, op-timism-about-life, altruism, Menschlichkeit, unity.

In an ideal world.

Tzedakah types of Mitzvahs are capable of producing peace, peace-of-mind, security. It is common ground and neutral ground, and all benefit: Tzedakah-actor as well as the beneficiary. At times I wonder just how much some of the infighting and conflict we experience might not be alleviated by joint Tzedakah projects. We see so many fine programs working with alcoholic people, poor people, battered spouses and children, etc., that cross all party lines. In my fantasy work, I think, "If half of the people would get the flu at one time, and the other half had to take care of them, and, once cured, both sides then switch positions, what would be the end result?"

In an ideal or fantasy world.

Once, at a public lecture where the audience included individuals from a broad spectrum of the Jewish community, I made mention of the fact that the Jewish battered women's shelter in one city had been started by the Mikveh women. These individuals who supervise the local ritual bath had seen bruises on some of the women who had come to perform their monthly immersions. They saw things no one else might know about and they responded with Ultimate Care. Thus began the program of shelter and refuge for the battered wives.

A few weeks later, my friend, Louise Cohen, who had been there, said, "Do you know at what moment you really 'had' the crowd?" I didn't recall any particular words I had said that had drawn the audience's particular interest and pulled them together, but Louise told me that it was when I mentioned the Mikveh women and the shelter. It seems that the Orthodox listeners took special note when they understood how this very human situation was managed in what appeared to be a purely ritual situation. It was a critical merging of the two realms, the human (one might say, the *very* human) and the ritual. The more liberal Jewish listeners, who according to the myth, supposedly have a corner on all social action-type Mitzvahs, were surprised that their right-wing counterparts had risen to the occasion, since they assumed (according to the myth), that their concerns extended no further than Kosher food, the infinite details of keeping the Sabbath, and other similar concerns.

In the real world, the theory doesn't quite work out in practice the way we would want it to. Whether or not that invalidates the theory should be left to the philosophers and theoreticians. At the very least, Jewish tradition offers a set of guidelines. At the very, very least we should recall the words of one of the Chassidic Rebbis, quoted by Martin Buber in *Ten Rungs*, "He who learns the Torah and is not troubled by it,...the worst scoundrel is better than he!" To study the Torah passionately, rather than simply coldly and dispassionately-for-the-sake-of-scholarship is a good starting point (though certainly there is a need for dispassionate scholarship, too.) Once the students' guts are churning and their minds are mind spinning — then there might be more action, leading to more peace and unity. Louise says that, at that point in the talk, there was a certain something in the air, certain walls were broken down, a communality of spirit and understanding pulled them together.

As I said, I was unaware of this. But I remember mentioning other such examples, specifically the issue of clothing for Jews who might need it. I explained that, in some cities where I had spoken, I posed the question, "Suppose you had 15 overcoats in perfectly good condition that you would like to get to other Jews. How would you find them?" I told the audience that in some of the cities the answer was clear: members of the Orthodox community would be able to distribute them, to non-Orthodox as well as Orthodox Jews. Their network was waiting to do it. So, too, with other specific Mitzvah-needs....There was not only a willingness to manage the mechanics of the Mitzvah, but a structure was already in place to carry out the mission. It was like a minor revelation to many people who were there.

There were no recriminations or accusations. I assume I was being descriptive rather than accusatory, explaining how — while so much of the interdenominational fighting has sprung from the Left accusing the Right of insensitivity — how the Left could overcome some of that hostility and, by joint effort, find some of this common ground which could get them working together. Working together in Tzedakah programs at least would cause some face-to-face communication and hand-to-hand contact, hopefully some more understanding, and maybe a little more peace.

In a fantasy world? In an ideal world?

Or is this the real world, at least some small, too-much-ignored part of the real world?

1.

Anav, Anvetan — *unassuming, humble*
Ruach Nemucha — *an unassuming personality*
Shefal Ruach — *unassuming, humble*
Byshan — *quiet, self-effacing*
Byshan Gadol — *very self-effacing*
Tam, Tamim — *innocent, simple*
Ish Kasher — *Mensch*
    Mehugan — *Menschlich, decent, fit as a human being*
Noach — *easy to get along with*
    Noach Lirtzot — *easily appeased*
    BeNichuta — *easily, softly, quietly*
    Ruach HaBriot Nocha Haymenu — *other people find that person pleasant*
Da'ato Me'Orevet Im HaBriot — *gets along well with others*
MeKubbal Al HaBriot — *well thought of by others*
Ma'avir Al Midotav — *having a non-insistent personality*
She'Ayno Ma'amid Al Midotav — *undemanding of personal Kavod, having a non-insistent personality*
Ahuv LeMa'ala VeNechmad LeMata — *beloved by Heaven and considered pleasant by other people*
HaNe'elavin VeAynan Olevin — *able to accept insults rather than insult others*

2.

Ga'ava — *arrogance*
Yohora — *arrogance*
Gassut HaRuach — *arrogance*
Zachut HaDa'at — *arrogance*
Chutzpa — *arrogance*
    Chutzpat Panim — *arrogance*
Azut Panim — *arrogance (literally: hard-facedness)*
Azut Metzach — *arrogance*
Mevayyesh — *one who embarrasses or humiliates*
LeVazot — *demean*
LeKalel — *demean, curse, treat with disrespect*
LeHachlim — *to demean, humiliate*
LeCharayf — *to abuse, insult*
Kapdan — *a person with a severe or irascible personality*
Ka'as — *anger*
Kin'ah — *jealousy*

List #1 is a partial gathering of positive personality terms from Rabbinic literature. Jewish tradition considers these to be desirable traits.

List #2 is a partial gathering of negative personality terms from Rabbinic literature. Jewish tradition considers these to be undesirable personal characteristics.

Many of these words appear in noun, verb, adjectival, and adverbial forms, giving them great flexibility and range.

Neither list is exhaustive. They were assembled over the course of preparing this book, as an attempt to discover just what kind of personality our teachers from the past deemed appropriate. In the specific contexts of our study (Dignity, Love, Peacemaking), it would be worthwhile to see how (if at all) each fits into the framework.

In the realm of peacemaking in daily life, is arrogance a better or worse trait than humility?

In the world of politics, is anger and abuse more appropriate (at least at times) than soft-spokenness and innocence?

Is it naive to think that relatively pure moral-grandeur-of-the-soul carries as much weight in confrontational situations as brute force?

Is list #1 synonymous with the recent slang term "wimpy"?

Is list #2 the more authentic one because it supposedly works better in the so-called Real World?

How do Lists #1 and #2 apply specifically to the areas of marriage, friendship, business, international relations?

Do we read List #1 and say, "Well, that's fine and good, but it just isn't realistic at all"?

For transgressions between human beings and God —
Yom Kippur provides atonement.

But between one human being and another —
Yom Kippur does not provide atonement
until the one person appeases the other.

(Mishna Yoma, Chapter 8, end)

This is a well-known passage, taken from Rabbinic Literature and mentioned in many Machzorim, the High Holiday prayerbooks.

Taking the text seriously would mean there would be a great onrush of letters and phone calls before Yom Kippur as Jews everywhere call and write to ask for personal forgiveness.

It happens.

And it is a fine example of how Halacha-Jewish law programs very specific human interaction into the calendar, offering everyone the opportunity to act, to make amends, to set things right.

In recent centuries, there was even a monthly practice called Yom Kippur Katan ("The Small Yom Kippur"), complete with fasting and special prayers.

My friend, Mark Stadler, offers the following suggestion: At the beginning of the Kol Nidray prayers on Yom Kippur evening, the Rabbi should invite the assembled congregants to take time *then and there* to pair off and step outside with those they may have wronged, and *then and there* ask for forgiveness.

Come and hear:

If a friend's pack animal needs to be unloaded
[because the cargo is too heavy for the animal],

and at the same time
an enemy's animal needs to be loaded up,

the Mitzvah is to load up the enemy's animal first.

This is so that the person might overcome
his or her inclination-to-do-the-unMenschlich thing [Yetzer HaRa].
(Bava Metzia 32b)

Pure Halacha-Jewish Law.

Because the loaded animal is straining under the excessive weight of the freight it is carrying, we might think that we should help unload that animal first....The other can wait. But, no, the Halacha states that — even considering the pain of the other animal — we must assist our enemy first, because we might otherwise just ignore that person completely, this enemy of ours, and thereby reinforce or even worsen the strained relations between us. The act of helping him load up the animal may, in fact, produce the exact opposite effect and break down whatever walls separate us.

These are the things for which people
enjoy the interest on their efforts in This World,
and for which the principal investment
remains intact in the Next World:

Honoring one's mother and father,
and performing acts of caring, loving kindness,
and making peace between one person and another
[Hava'at Shalom Bayn Adam LeChavayro],

and Torah study is equal to all of them.

(Mishna Pe'ah 1:1)

"...and making peace between one person and another": While none of us is certain about what the rewards in the Next World might be, the "interest" in This World is most certainly a more decent life for everyone.

According to *Roget's Thesaurus*, among the opposite words for "peace" are: war, combat, hostilities, hostility, cold war, war of nerves, psychological warfare, dissension, conflict, friction, strife, fractiousness, quarrelsomeness, altercation, disharmony, discord, misunderstanding, quarreling, fighting, dispute, bickering, brawling, estrangement, rupture, schism, battle, struggle — to name a few.

A world with peace and without Roget's partial list is certainly one wherein our investments produce enormous returns.

1.
Though your beginnings be small,
in the end, things will flourish greatly.

(Job 8:7)

2.
Rava said:

When a person is brought to Final Judgment,
he or she will be asked,
"....
Did you expect the positive outcome of things?"

(Shabbat 31a)

Text #1 is a standard sermonic reference to modest beginnings that lead to great successes. In the area of peacemaking, it is hoped that a little work here, some more effort there, and joint action in a third place, a fourth place, a hundredth, will produce great results.

The second text needs some linguistic explanation. "Did you expect" in the Hebrew is "Tzipita" — which carries the following range of meanings: expect, hope for, look to, anticipate, eagerly await (much as the word "esperar" means in Spanish). "Hoping for", on the one hand, has a bit of a passive nuance, whereas "expect" carries more of an active connotation, i.e., "Did you expect positive results to happen as a result of your efforts?" "The positive outcome of things" is "Yeshu'ah" in Hebrew, which can mean: "ultimate salvation" (not personal salvation), in the sense of a decent world to live in, a better life for others as a result of your actions.

The Talmudic question then means something like this: Did you actively pursue the appropriate actions in life that would bring about a more dignified, loving, caring, and peaceful world, and did you live your life hoping-for-and-expecting that this could, indeed, happen?

Jewish tradition believes that our efforts are not fruitless, but rather, with concerted human labors for the good of the world and humanity, the world will not remain forever the same, but will move towards better times for all humankind.

CONFLICT RESOLUTION

The story goes that, not so long ago somewhere in the Middle East, a certain scorpion said to a certain camel, "Let me hop on your back, and you can give me a ride across the river. I cannot swim, but since you can, you can help me." The camel replied, "I know your tricks — once we get halfway across, you'll sting me, and I'll die." "That's silly," the scorpion replied. "If you die, then I'll drown!" The camel (with his camel intelligence) grasped the solid reasoning of the scorpion, and since, he, too, wanted to get to the other side of the river, he said, "Hop on!" The camel started swimming across, when — somewhere around the halfway point — the scorpion stung him. Disappointed, surprised, and definitely confused, the camel said (as he began to sink), "See what a stupid thing you've done. Now we're both going to die!" The scorpion responded (as he, too, began to sink), "Look, this is the Middle East, isn't it?"

The following section does not attempt to cover all the human situations where conflict arises: war and peace, internal strife, divorce mediation, parent-child relations. The few selections I have chosen may not even be relevant to most of them, but they are recorded us a point of departure for understanding some of the Jewish principles of compromise and conflict resolution, plus a couple of examples of Talmudic stories that involved conflict-and-resolution.

The examples involving Hillel and Rabbi Elazar the son of Rabbi Shimon are presented as exercises for Torah students in comparing how they would react in certain situations with how the Rabbis reacted. There are many methods used nowadays to change the course and mode of human actions — from behavior modification to arbitration to lawsuits to any one of a number of other approaches. After studying this section, it is hoped that the student would have a clearer sense of where and when each method might be appropriate, and how to set up the mechanics of arbitration and mediation boards or courts-with-clout therapy, whenever and wherever necessary.

Rabbi Eliezer the son of Rabbi Yossi HaGlili says:

Using arbitration to settle a dispute [as opposed to going to court]
is prohibited.

Rabbi Yehoshua ben Korcha says:
It is a Mitzvah to use arbitration.
. . . .

One would think that where there is Justice
there is no Peace,
and where there is Peace,
there is no Justice.

What would be a kind of Justice
where there is also Peace?

One would say:
arbitration.
. . . .
Furthermore,
anywhere there is Justice,
there is no Tzedakah,
Tzedakah — there is no Justice.

Then what kind of Justice
also has an element of Tzedakah?

One would say:
arbitration.

(Sanhedrin 6b)

Rabbi Eliezer the son of Rabbi Yossi HaGlili is emphatically opposed to
methods of arbitration and mediation because pure Justice is not served. The set-
tlement will not be completely Just because both sides give up something they think
is absolutely rightfully theirs. Therefore, arbitration/mediation is wrong in-and-of-
itself.

Rabbi Yehoshua ben Korcha sees it differently: people are people, society
must function, and there must be peace and Tzedakah (probably meaning something
like "decent interpersonal relations" in this context) as part of the basic and critical
process of human Justice.

The Talmud uses two terms for arbitration/mediation: Bitzu'a and Peshara.
A thorough study of both terms, where they overlap and where they diverge — and

how they developed through the centuries of Jewish legal literature — would be most beneficial nowadays. It would help us understand better in which situations law courts would be appropriate forums, and on the other hand, when other methods might possibly provide better solutions. The renewed study of this material could lead to the establishment of more arbitration boards and courts-of-high-integrity. We know that, in certain earlier periods of Jewish history, the Batay Din courts had the power to enforce their decisions. Outside of Israel, this is rarely true in the Jewish community, except in certain places where a Bet Din or some arbitration/mediation mechanism has been established. Some national Jewish organizations also have such institutions. As in the secular courts and arbitration/mediation boards, these institutions must, of course, be above factionalism and politics.

For so many issues today, the question is one of recourse: where can proper satisfaction be achieved, either Justice or Justice-with-Peace-and-Tzedakah?

Other issues include integrity and principle and the fear of surrender and compromise and unfairness.

In one area, however, the question is not, "Do we hold on to our principles and personal integrity?" but rather "*How* do we hold on to our principles and personal integrity?"

Does everyone sell out at one time or another?

If everyone sells out, are the differences in the price merely quantitative, or is the quality of the person's integrity totally compromised?

Are all politics dirty and degrading?

Are politics *by nature* dirty and degrading?

Is there room for any Menschlichkeit in politics?

Do we leave our Jewish principles outside the door when we get to the so-called "real issues" of life, conveniently compartmentalizing, leaving Judaism to operate only in certain areas and putting it aside, out of range, for others?

Hard questions.

Real questions.

It once happened that Rabbi Elazar the son of Rabbi Shimon
was coming from his teacher's house in Migdal Gedor.

He was riding on a donkey alongside a river
and feeling very proud of himself
because he had studied a great deal of Torah.

Along the way,
he happened to meet a man who was extremely ugly.

The man said,
"Shalom to you, my teacher."

But Rabbi Elazar the son of Rabbi Shimon
did not reply to his greeting.
Instead, he said,
"How ugly is 'that man'!
Is everyone in your city as ugly as you are?"

The man replied,
"I don't know
but go and say to the Craftsperson who made me,
'How ugly is this utensil you have made!'"

When Rabbi Elazar the son of Rabbi Shimon
realized he had done wrong,
he dismounted from the donkey and said,
"I humble myself before you.
Forgive me."

The man said to him,
"I will not forgive you
until you go to the Craftsperson who made me, and say,
'How ugly is this utensil you have made!'"

The rabbi continued walking behind him
until they came to the Rabbi's city.

The townspeople came out,
calling out greetings, saying,
"Shalom to you,
My Rabbi, my Rabbi,
my teacher, my teacher!"

The man said,
"Whom are you calling,
'My Rabbi, my Rabbi'?"

They said to him,
"We are speaking of this person
who is walking behind you."

The man said,
"If this one is a rabbi,
I hope there will not be many more like him
among the Jews."

They said to him,
"Why is that?"

He said to them,
"He did such-and-such a thing to me."

They said to him,
"Nevertheless, forgive him,
because he is a great person for his Torah-knowledge."

He said to them,
"For your sakes I will forgive him,
but do not let him get into the habit of doing such things."

Rabbi Elazar the son of Rabbi Shimon
immediately went into the place of Torah-study
and taught,

"A person should always be as soft as a reed
and not as hard as a cedar.

It is because of this quality
that reeds have been privileged to be selected
as pens with which Torahs, Tfillin, and Mezuzot are written."

(Ta'anit 20a-b)

This story from the 2nd Century is very troubling. We are at a loss to understand what triggered Rabbi Elazar the son of Rabbi Shimon's cruel reaction to the man's innocent greeting.

Was it because he was so lost in the Upper Worlds of High Torah that he had forgotten all sense of life on an everyday level? Was his understanding of the abstract beauty of those Upper Worlds of Torah so dazzling that he was blinded to common realities?

Was it simply the Rabbi's personality flaw, a streak of irascibility that he had not yet conquered?

Was it simply that the encounter was so sudden and unexpected that the rabbi blurted out his nasty line before he had a chance to think?

Whatever the motivation, the victim throws the rabbi off balance by demanding he consider the greater implications of what he has said. Rather than take personal offense, he places the problem in a larger context: God must be at fault if I am so unpleasant looking.

More questions:

Is the ugly man *too* demanding? Should he not have accepted Rabbi Elazar the son of Rabbi Shimon's apology immediately?

Why would he make the rabbi go through such an involved process of making amends?

And when he finally *did* forgive the Rabbi, it seems to be for the wrong reason: he forgives him for the sake of the townspeople, and not for the Rabbi's own sake.

And yet another question:

Why did the ugly man say, "Do not let him get into the habit of doing such things"? Why didn't he say, "Don't ever let him do it again"? Was his answer more realistic, and would it have been too much to ask that, after this one incident, he would so radically change his personality that it would never happen again.

So many questions.

But one thing is clear: the closing images of the reed and the cedar are very striking. In the Bible, cedars are always used as positive symbols — they are mighty, magnificent and breathtakingly beautiful, particularly the Cedars of Lebanon. In our tale, the ugly man has said, "It may be that they are mighty, magnificent, and beautiful, but they are of no use in the presence of challenge. They do not have the resilience of the humble reed that knows how to bend in the wind."

Our Rabbis have taught:

One should always be as unassuming as Hillel,
and not as irascible as Shammai.

It once happened that two people made the following bet:
Whoever makes Hillel angry will win 400 Zuz.

One of them said,
"I will make Hillel angry."

It was Friday afternoon,
and Hillel was shampooing his hair.

The man went to Hillel's house and shouted,
"Anybody here named Hillel?
Anybody here named Hillel?"

Hillel put on a robe and went out to see him.

He said,
"My son,
what is it that you want?"

The man replied,
"I have a question to ask."

Hillel said,
"Ask my son. Ask."

"Why do Babylonians* have such [unpleasantly] rounded heads?"

Hillel said to him,
"My son, you have asked a great question.
It is because their midwives are not very skilled."

The man went away and waited a while.

Then he came back and shouted,
"Is anybody here named Hillel?
Is anybody here named Hillel?"

*Hillel was a Babylonian by birth.

Hillel put on a robe and went out to see him.

He said to him,
"My son,
what is it that you want?"

He said to him,
"I have a question to ask"

Hillel said,
"Ask, my son. Ask."

"Why do Palmyrans have such drippy eyes?"

Hillel said to him,
"My son, you have asked a great question.
It is because they live in sandy places."

The man went away and waited a while.

Then he came back again and shouted,
"Anybody here named Hillel?
Anybody here named Hillel?"

Hillel put on a robe and went out to see him.

He said to him,
"My son, what is it that you want?"

He said to him,
"I have a question to ask."

Hillel said,
"Ask, my son. Ask."

"Why do Africans have such wide feet?"

Hillel said to him,
"My son, you have asked a great question.
It is because they live in swampy places."

The man said to Hillel,
"I have many questions to ask,

but I am afraid that you will get angry."

Hillel wrapped himself up well in his robe
and sat down before the man, saying,
"Any and all questions you might have to ask — ask them."

The man said,
"Are you the Hillel everyone calls 'Prince of Israel'?"

Hillel replied,
"Yes I am."

The man said,
"If you are he,
I hope there are not many more like you among the Jews!"

Hillel said,
"My son, why is that?"

He answered,
"Because I just lost 400 Zuz because of you."

Hillel replied,
"It is better that you lose 400 Zuz —
and even another 400 —
than for Hillel to get angry."

(Shabbat 30b-31a)

This tale is a paradigm of interpersonal tensions and the conflict relief. It contains all kinds of wonderful elements: the pre-Shabbat-preparation rush in the air, the earthiness of Hillel's shampooing his hair (one can easily visualize the suds), the familiar obnoxiousness of the Nudnik....

I leave the in-depth discussion of this story to the reader.

CLOSING PRAYER FOR PEACE

When Rav would conclude his Standing Prayer,
he would recite the following:

May it be Your will, O Lord, our God,
*   to give us a long life,*
a life of peace,
*   a life of goodness,*
a life of blessing,
*   a life of decent livelihood,*
a life of good health,
*   a life lived fearing wrongdoing,*
a life that has no embarrassment and humiliation,
*   a life rich with dignity,*
a life in which we will be filled with love of the Torah
*   and the Awe of Heaven,*
a life in which You will fill all our hearts' desires
*   for goodness.*

(Berachot 16b)

GLOSSARY

Aggada (H): the narrative, non-legal portions of Rabbinic Literature.

Eretz Yisrael (H): the Land of Israel.

Gemara (Aramaic): the latter portion of the Talmud.

Halacha (H): Jewish Law; also a specific Jewish law.

Lehavdil (H, lit. "To differentiate"): said when making a comparison between two different categories of things.

Machzor (H): the High Holiday prayerbook.

Mashiach (H): the Messiah.

Mensch (Y, adj., Menschlich; abs., Menschlichkeit): a decent, caring human being.

Mikveh (H): a ritual bath.

Mishna (H): the earlier section of the Talmud.

Momzer (Y, adj.=Momzerish): a bastard, s.o.b.

Negev (H): the southern portion of Israel, originally a desert, now blooming.

Nudnik (Y): a bothersome person.

Pirke Avot (h, lit. "Chapters of the Ancestors"): a section of the Mishna consisting of ethical maxims.

Purim (H): joyous holiday celebrating the victory of the Jews over the wicked Haman in ancient Persian times.

Shabbat (H, Y=Shabbas): the Sabbath.

Siddur (H): the prayerbook.

Talmud (H): extensive compendium of discussions, tales, aphorisms, and insights from Jewish academies (Yeshivot) during the first five centuries of the Common Era.

Tzaddik (H): a Righteous person.

Tzedakah (H, lit., "Justice, doing the right thing"): the Jewish way of giving.

Yom Kippur (H): the Day of Atonement.

Zeyde (Y): grandfather.

DANNY SIEGEL is a free-lance author, poet, and lecturer who resides in Rockville, Maryland, when not on his speaking tours or in Israel distributing Tzedakah monies. He is the author of five books of poetry, four of which are now out of print, as well as three anthologies of his selected writings.

In this current work, *Family Reunion: Making Peace in the Jewish Community,* Danny Siegel addresses a painful subject . . . disunity and polarization. This book is an attempt to bring to light sources which are a part of classical Jewish literature, and which could be of use in any attempt to restore harmony.

Danny is the author of a book of essays and three anthologies on the subject of Midrash and Halachah, now combined into a single volume. He is also co-author with Allan Gould of a book of Jewish humor, and tapes of his poetry readings and humor presentations have been produced.

The publication of *Gym Shoes and Irises. Book Two,* rounded out Danny's devotion to the "how-to" of personalized Tzedakah begun many years before the issuance of the first *Gym Shoes and Irises* in 1982. Another volume: *Munbaz II and Other Mitzvah Heroes* (1988) was another major contribution by Danny Siegel in recognizing the deeds of loving-kindness by the good people of this world.

Siegel is a popular lecturer at synagogues, Jewish federations, community centers, conventions, and retreats, where he teaches Tzedakah and Jewish values and recites from his works. His books and talks have received considerable acclaim throughout the entire North American Jewish community.